Thrivi...

at

school

To the kids and parents of today, who will
help our teachers shape the minds of tomorrow.

Thriving
at
school

*A practical guide to help your child
enjoy the crucial school years*

Dr John Irvine and John Stewart

FINCH PUBLISHING
SYDNEY

Thriving at school: A practical guide to help your child enjoy the crucial school years

First published in 2000 in Australia and New Zealand by Simon & Schuster. This edition published in 2008 by Finch Publishing Pty Limited, ABN 49 057 285 248, P O Box 120, Lane Cove, NSW 1595, Australia.

12 11 10 09 08   8 7 6 5 4 3 2 1

The National Library of Australia Cataloguing-in-Publication entry:

Irvine, John (John Forsyth), 1942–
Thriving at school : a practical guide to help your child
enjoy the crucial school years /authors, Dr John Irvine ; John Stewart.
2nd ed.
Lane Cove, N.S.W. : Finch Publishing, 2008.
9781876451837 (pbk.)
Includes index.

1. Home and school. 2. Child rearing. 3. Readiness for school.
Other Authors: Stewart, John (John Douglas), 1967–

155.424

Edited by Sean Doyle
Editorial assistance by Rosemary Peers
Text typeset in Stone serif and Futura by Emtype Desktop Publishing
Cover design by Natalie Bowra
Cover photo courtesay of iStock International Inc
Internal illustrations by Roy Bisson
Printed by Brown Prior Anderson

Notes   The 'Notes' section at the back of this book contains useful additional information and references to quoted material in the text. Each reference is linked to the text by its relevant page number and an identifying line entry.

Disclaimer   While every care has been taken in researching and compiling the information in this book, it is in no way intended to replace professional legal advice and counselling. Readers are encouraged to seek such help as they deem necessary. The authors and publisher specifically disclaim any liability arising from the application of information in this book.

Finch titles can be viewed and purchased at www.finch.com.au

Advance praise for this book

Practical, detailed and wide ranging, the authors' experience with kids and schools shines through.

Steve Biddulph, author of *Raising Boys* and *Manhood*

Parents of infants and primary students will draw great benefit from this well structured and accessible manual, rich in experience, reassurance and common sense. The authors understand the vital importance of parents and teachers working together.

Andrew Mullins, Headmaster of Redfield College,
author of *Parenting For Character*

This book provides a great overview for parents on how to help kids thrive. A must read.

Andrew Fuller, clinical psychologist, family therapist and
author of *Tricky Kids*

Full of sound, practical information based on good research, common sense and the authors' extensive experience. It will help parents in setting up a more positive school experience for their children. Highly recommended.

John Cooper, senior clinical psychologist

Thriving at School is an invaluable resource for parents who want to maximise their child's chance of learning to their best potential whilst building a strong sense of positive self-esteem. The book provides a powerhouse of Top Tips, Checklists and To Dos/Not to Dos for motivated parents to best support their kids. Most importantly, parents will learn cutting edge information about the importance of values, attitudes and habits, how to appreciate differences in intelligence and learning styles and how to keep up with and protect your children from bullies and cyber-trouble.

Dr Janet Hall, author of *Fight-free Families* and *Fear-free Children*

Both Dr John Irvine and John Stewart are great advocates for children and promote a holistic approach that involves the family and the community including schools as a major part of today's society. This book is a testament to both authors' experience in their work with children and the power of humour to inform readers of the issues surrounding thriving at school.

Marilyn Barnes, National Director, Home-Start

Contents

Introduction

Thriving at School strives to help children flourish in the crucial school years and beyond – and to unlock the school gate for parents. Current research shows that success in life is not founded primarily on IQ (the 'Intelligence Quotient' as we have conventionally understood it) but rather on 'EQ' – our Emotional intelligence Quotient (see page 52). This refers to our ability to be more understanding of others and more successful in relationships, which produces a positive outlook on life. Nowadays, developing emotional intelligence is an important goal in education, and we discuss it in this book. Similarly, we have distilled our approach, which builds on this understanding, into what we call 'The VAH model' – the Values, Attitudes and Habits that enable a young school-goer (who may be hesitant and insecure) to emerge with the resilience, confidence, creativity and flexibility necessary to thrive in the twenty-first century (see pages 28–51).

Thriving at School is focused on helping parents and teachers produce a child who has the qualities to cope with a changing world. When today's children emerge from school, the majority of jobs on offer will be vastly different to those available now. In a world where change is one of the few certainties, our VAH model provides the backbone to help parents and teachers produce a confident and competent learner capable of successfully tackling that brave new world.

The traditional '3Rs' – reading, 'riting and 'rithmetic – are still neces-sary, but they're not enough on their own to ensure our children thrive as learners. What our kids also need are the values of respect, respon-sibility and relationships – the new 3Rs. These values underpin every student's capacity to thrive at school.

This book is an accessible, practical guide for parents to the many stages of their child's life at 'big' school. It covers the key 'start-up' issues such as how to choose a good school, preparing for the crucial first day, and the skills that a child should have before walking through those school gates. We then present our VAH model, and outline how a child can thrive both as a learner and in the classroom (no, they're not the same thing). Following that, we lift the lid on the socially demanding world of the playground, and offer advice on how to help kids thrive with others, as well as how to cope with the challenges of loneliness and the many (and new) forms of bullying. We then survey the 'crossroads', the nexus point where the school meets the home – and where many key issues play out. These include helping the family cope with homework, assignments, schoolwork-related computer usage, teachers' reports, requests for interviews, difficulties with teachers, excursions, and most other common or conceivable topics.

And we present all this in easy-to-digest, bite-sized chunks.

Thriving at school doesn't happen by chance or by accident. It happens when we get that magic combination of switched-on teachers, supportive parents and enthusiastic learners. And then it's a truly beautiful thing to behold.

In a nutshell, then, the key features of our book are:

❖ useful links to a purpose-built *Thriving at School* website for further information on specific topics
❖ a detailed discussion of the use of computers in education
❖ strategies to handle bullying, the new menace of cyber-bullying and, of course, discrimination in any form
❖ significant attention not only to the traditional 3Rs, but also to the new 3Rs of respect, responsibility and relationships – and to the values, attitudes and habits that underpin school performance, and
❖ perhaps the most comprehensive coverage that any educational handbook devotes to the vital home–school issues, because an effective interplay between these two hemispheres of a child's world is the bedrock upon which an education is built.

We hope that this exciting new edition offers the guidance parents seek to help them ensure that their child is well and truly 'thriving at school'.

Dr John Irvine & John Stewart
March 2008

Note: In the interests of fairness, we use 'he' and 'she' in alternating Parts of this book when talking about non-specific children.

Prologue: Choosing the right school

Choosing the right school, so your child can thrive, is vital – especially as more choice is now available to parents than perhaps ever before. The best idea is to look at the children already going to the target school, listen to their parents, and try to get a feeling about the place.

As a general rule, schools are what you make of them. And, as another general rule, young children are better off at their neighbourhood school, where they can build up an in-school and out-of-school network of friends. Travelling far to and from school daily and then having no-one familiar nearby to play with, unless a parent performs a complex shuttle service, can be a bit stressful for everyone concerned.

What to look for

Look for some of these features, but don't expect all of them! If you score on more than half, you've found a good school:

❖ Preschool children are invited to at least one Orientation Day before starting.
❖ The school is close to home and/or is easily accessible.
❖ Your child's friends from preschool and/or neighbourhood are also starting school there.
❖ Students look reasonably happy going into the school (and better, if they look reasonably happy coming out!).
❖ School entrances are busy, chatty places.
❖ Most kids wear the school uniform where uniforms are a school rule.
❖ The school has an active clothing pool.
❖ The school has taken steps to help the kids avoid skin cancer, such as prescribing wide-brimmed hats in summer (maybe even sunglasses) or having plenty of shade areas.
❖ The children at play look busy and happy, and the teachers on playground duty seem interested and involved with them.

- ❖ Teachers' cars are in the carpark well before the start of school.
- ❖ The school secretaries are warm, friendly and helpful.
- ❖ The school has a clear welfare or pastoral care policy.
- ❖ Parents are involved in school affairs.
- ❖ The school rules are simple, clearly stated, positive and well-enforced.
- ❖ You've heard good things about the school.
- ❖ The principal and teachers seem keen to meet parents and involve them in school activities.
- ❖ There is the opportunity to join special after-school or lunchtime groups or activities.
- ❖ Reports of the school's success appear in the local media.
- ❖ The school grounds and buildings are well presented and clean.
- ❖ The library is well stocked, open and inviting.
- ❖ There are lots of resources, like computer banks, sporting and musical instruments.
- ❖ The school canteen is clean, sells mostly healthy food, and the helpers are friendly.
- ❖ There are special provisions for children with physical or learning difficulties.
- ❖ Classrooms are generally attractive and busy with activity and colour.
- ❖ Kids and teachers greet each other both in and out of school.

Single-sex or co-educational?

If your child is a girl, this section is probably of little importance, but if you have a son, then the facts need to be clear. We've known for years that at school entry (five years old), girls are developmentally on average about six months ahead of boys. Every infants teacher will testify that girls, on average, are more ready to settle at schoolwork, to cope with sitting at a desk, and to identify with school learning. And it's now common knowledge that girls outstrip the boys on academic criteria for most of their school lives.

Researcher Georgia Kamperos has found that 'boys and girls achieved better results when they attended single-sex schools'. Of course, Ms Kamperos was not looking at such non-academic issues as social skills, attitudes to the opposite sex, values, self-confidence, communication skills, self-image, etc.; anecdotal evidence indicates that co-educated students are often more mature in some of these areas. Nevertheless, it may be that you need to examine the possibility, if not of single-sex schools, then maybe of single-sex classes in some areas, at some levels. From our review of the research and from our experience, we would advocate as follows:

❖ In primary school there is probably more advantage in co-education. Children need to learn to mix and feel confident with the opposite sex. Although girls are outperforming boys academically, there are distinct emotional and social reasons why mixed classes do well in terms of general development.

❖ Check that your school has a reasonable ratio of males on staff. Boys need good male role models, but the ratio generally in primary is about five female to one male teacher.

❖ If your child is attending a co-educational school, it is preferable that there are some separate play areas for girls, as research finds that girls are much more active in play when they are not competing with boys for play space. This doesn't mean that there should not be some shared play space as well.

❖ If your son is attending a co-educational school, check with the principal as to what provisions exist for support services. Like it or not, boys often do not thrive at school as well as girls. We're not just talking about academic matters – boys are outstripping girls quite severely in learning difficulties, behaviour problems, suspensions, expulsions, truancies, playground injuries, fights, referrals to counsellors, or whatever criteria of concern you'd like to pose.

❖ Check with the principal that boys are well integrated in leadership roles and contribute to extra-curricular activities as much as girls do. If so, you have a very good school for boys; the general pattern is that girls are much more involved in leadership, debating, performing, choir, orchestra, use of library, public speaking ... and the list goes on. Boys generally are much less motivated to step up into such roles when competing with girls.

Keep in mind that your child is highly unlikely to enter a single-sex tertiary institution or workplace – and after all, this is what we are preparing him for.

Public or private school?

For some families, few choices carry more significance or symbolism than the selection of public or private schooling for their children. Australian parents are drifting towards private schools in increasing numbers – maybe because they think they can have more say in their child's education, or because certain private schools have beliefs or values that some parents feel are starting to be eroded in the public system, or because families have more disposable income and fewer kids to educate, or maybe because they see the enormous pressures on public education.

For whatever reason there has been an increase of about 18,000 students (1.6 percent) per year in private school enrolments, compared to a 0.1 percent increase for public schools.

One of the most common mistakes is for parents to opt for some prestigious school because of its reputation, and take little account of its expectations (e.g. religious), its policies, resources, facilities, curriculum or standards. As a result, the whole family ends up feeling like square pegs in round holes.

One strong suggestion is that parents write down a shopping list of their educational requirements and beliefs. This will clarify what you really want for your child.

Teacher says ...

I am a public school teacher with one child at public primary and one at private high school. The private school has been good for my son's sense of self-worth because no-one picks on him for wanting to study and do well in his work. But my other son will probably stay in the public system because he's more sporty, wants to stay with his mates, and is keen on the more practical subjects that the local high school has to offer. I suppose it all boils down to 'horses for courses'.

Key factors

❖ Per capita, private schools tend to perform a little better in the Year 12 Certificate, but there's also other research which suggests that at university level public school students are better survivors – maybe because they've had to learn independent survival skills earlier on.

❖ Any religious or other family moral commitments must rank high in the decision-making process, as school is meant to be an extension of, not in competition with, a family's values.

❖ Finance can be a big issue. Remember that being able to afford to send a child to private school is not just a matter of paying the fees, it also involves all the peripheral costs. As a rule of thumb, budget on twice the school fees.

❖ Forcing kids to attend a particular school against their will can be a disaster; if the kids don't enjoy being at the school, you won't enjoy the reports.

❖ By far the most important considerations are the practical ones such as transport, uniforms, friendships and such basic issues as whether you can afford to do the same thing for your other kids.

Part One

1

Is your **child** really ready?

'So ... be your name Buxbaum or Bixby or Bray
Or Mordecai Ali Van Allen O'Shea,
You're off to Great Places!
Today is your day!
Your mountain is waiting.
So ... get on your way!'

Dr Seuss

The 'great transition' is how we describe the move from preschool or childcare to 'big school' – the moment when you pass your most prized possession into the hands of the education system. This is the start of a 12- or 13-year journey. Strap yourself in! And remember back – re-live your own first day, with all its jangled nerves and bursting excitement.

You are about to celebrate your child 'growing so old so quick'. But one nagging question that many parents ask is: is my child too young for primary school? Thriving from the very start of school relies perhaps more on the parents than on the child. This Part will cover what you have to know, what you have to do, and what your child should be able to do, too.

And we will help answer those other important questions – What can I expect? How do I make my children winners? How do I separate from them if they get upset?

Too young to start?

Every year, we see parents who want to rush their kids on before they are ready. We just wish they'd put the kids' needs first.

Early-childhood teachers consistently and unanimously suggest that parents should not send their children to 'big school' if they're young and not ready. Parents can ask early-childhood staff about their child's readiness before making the big decision.

Infants teachers would be the first to state that whereas you can be too young to start school, you can never be too old (unless you are looking at kindergarten when well into your teens!).

What's the right age?

Present policies point to either four years and six months or four years and eight months as the most likely minimum age to start school. However, there are variations between States. Check with your State's education department for more specific information.

There is no evidence that starting later impacts adversely on learning. It is important that parents understand the difference between chronological age and developmental age. Just because a child turns five does not mean he or she has the maturity to handle the routines and expectations of big school.

No matter what age, there will remain the 'kindy phenomenon' of having 12 months separating the eldest from the youngest in a year. For some parents this will cause the first major case of school stress – having your pride and joy being described as 'immature' or 'would do much better if we could get him to sit!' Give your child time to settle and adjust, and don't be at all upset if it is suggested that your child repeat an infants grade. Kids adjust quickly. Keep in mind that some countries (e.g. in Scandinavia) don't start their children at school until they're six or even eight years old. In other countries, children attend for only half a day. The students they produce are not inferior; it's more a question of cultural preference.

A true tale ... the shock of school

Judy's six-year-old Jake is a good kid. He loves fixing up his bike, drawing, building and sport, and he plays and mixes well. But since starting school he has struggled with reading, and when Judy attended the parent–teacher night and mentioned how good he was at concentrating, his teacher's mouth dropped like she had swallowed a ghost. At school his behaviour is immature, he can't concentrate, he's flitty and easily distracted – and what did Judy think about repeating him next year? Now, has Judy got Jake wrong, or has the school?

Neither. Young Jake is very mature in 'right-brain work' (practicalities), but put him in the left-brain classroom amidst a wordy, busy avalanche of abstract ideas, and it's a different story. It could be that he can't keep up or can't keep listening in multi-track; or, if he has ADD/ADHD, he can't stay concentrated on the topics at hand because his brain keeps being sidetracked. Whichever is the case, six can be a good age to repeat a child if he's a bit young for his class – and be very careful how you explain this matter to him.

Great change means great risk

A leading expert in child development, Urie Bronfenbrenner, says that children are at greatest risk at times of greatest change. That could mean the change from home to preschool, or from preschool to school. At these times, kids' security is shaken; they are at their most nervous. If things go wrong from the start, then expect their normal fussing to turn into fears or even phobias as minor problems become catastrophes, and molehills turn into mountains overnight. So first impressions are very important, particularly for sensitive children. But for any child, a new start can be helped or hindered by what we do or don't do.

Teacher says ...

Another year in daycare is another year to roll in the mud, remove the garden rocks to find the slaters, and develop social skills in a nurturing environment. Some children just need a little more time before coming to school.

A true tale ... too much too young

One family was intent on sending their son (who was a lovely child) to big school because he was big, although he was only four. We strongly advised against the move because we didn't feel he was ready. Soon after starting, the problems began to surface. The teacher couldn't cope with his egocentric nature (young children have more awareness of themselves than others). Being at big school, with a class of other children all focusing on more structured learning, just wasn't working out – and it wasn't his fault. The parents were advised to withdraw him, so he came back to daycare, had a fabulous year. and is now doing really well in primary because he is mentally and socially ready.

What should you say before they start school?

Whatever you say, it needs to be positive. Children are very quick to pick up on parents' anxieties. And more often than not, it is the parents who have greater worries about their littlies leaving the nest. Kids are mostly very excited to start school – they see it as a move to become a 'big' person. They always want to be that little bit older. It is not uncommon for kids to be dressed, up and ready, sitting in the car and honking the horn at 6 a.m. ... at least on the first day! Three weeks into term, and you may find your child asking whether they have to 'go back again, every day'.

What should you do the year before?

There are a lot of routines that children have to follow at school. Don't wait until your child is starting school to establish routines with regard to bedtime, meal times, reading, and waking up in the morning. If these routines are established before starting school, the transition to big school will be so much easier: your child will cope with the discipline and the structure of the school day.

What your child should be able to do

Here's a list of the key *social skills* your child should have:

- ❖ mixes happily with friends at preschool
- ❖ has begun having friends over to play
- ❖ can go to preschool or parties without tears
- ❖ can stay within behavioural boundaries
- ❖ can share and take turns
- ❖ has best friends, and can talk about them in conversation
- ❖ can talk to adults other than just parents and close family, and
- ❖ has had extended periods of time away from parents.

Your child should have these key *educational abilities*:

- ❖ can draw people with three or four recognisable features
- ❖ has some control when colouring in
- ❖ can print or almost print own first name
- ❖ can talk in proper sentences, not just in two- or three-word phrases
- ❖ her speech is understandable, although it doesn't have to be perfect
- ❖ can remember parts of favourite books and re-tell known stories
- ❖ enjoys using a computer and is developing basic skills of controlling the mouse, etc.

- ❖ can repeat some nursery rhymes and/or finger plays
- ❖ can sing some kindergarten songs
- ❖ enjoys looking at pictures or listening to stories, and
- ❖ can count own fingers.

And your child should be managing these key *areas of independence*:

- ❖ is toilet-trained
- ❖ can dress self, including buttons
- ❖ can cut and paste with ease

- ❖ can open food packets, lunchboxes and drink bottles, and unwrap plastic-wrapped lunches
- ❖ can care for belongings
- ❖ knows basic colours and shapes
- ❖ can follow two simple instructions given together
- ❖ wants to learn, e.g. asks 'Why?' or 'How do you write ...?', and
- ❖ can stay at an activity for at least 10–15 minutes (if the child has not had any preschool experience).

A true tale ... worlds collide

A teacher had his daughter attending the school he worked at. As Dad, he had a meeting with the daughter's kindy teacher. The teacher offered to show the proud dad his daughter's work. The teacher-dad looked around, then later that evening arrived home to greet his little girl in the bath. He said, 'Darling, I met your teacher today and she showed me some of your work.'

His daughter stared at him and frowned: 'What are you doing in MY world?'

Children love the independence of their 'own' world. Parents will never share totally all that happens there – and should not expect to.

Teacher says ...

Be positive about school. If you are enthusiastic about your child and the school, then there's every chance that home and school will make a happy and productive partnership. Many parents fall into the trap of comparing their child to others in the class. Don't! Praise your child's individual efforts even if they might not be as good as you would like. Children start school at different developmental stages.

Be patient – children will get there in the end. It is not a race. A plant that grows quickly doesn't necessarily have better flowers.

The 'big' day

In a nutshell: find out where your child's classroom is situated. Be available to drop off and pick up your child, and be on time. Meet the teacher. Give your child time to unwind after school. Encourage your child to talk about school (e.g. who she played with, what story was read, what the other kids brought for lunch ...) but don't nag. Talk to other parents.

What to expect on the first morning

Chaos! Pure wonderful chaos – of emotions, new understandings, new faces and new opportunities. Children for 'kindy' (Year 1 in some systems) will usually come to school on their first day later than older children. Usually new 'buddies' are waiting to show their respect and an opportunity to care. Your child's eyes will be wide open ... and it will all be a bit too much (for mums and dads). This is the big day!

Now comes the moment of detachment. Some children will cry ... scream ... grab hold of furniture. Kindy or Year 1 teachers – that special breed – expect this. Parents, however, can feel quite embarrassed and can want to intervene. Don't. Kindy teachers know how to deal with such delicate situations. They will advise you to leave your child in the good hands of the teachers. They may need to hold your child, and distract her for a short period of time, giving parents the chance to leave. Always say goodbye and never leave without your child knowing. The teacher will call if things don't settle but, nearly always, as soon as you are gone, your child starts to smile and mix with others. These are the first steps on the path to 'being big'.

Remember, too, that most separation anxiety problems stem from the parents' anxiety, so if you're anxious, maybe go as a foursome with a friend and their child.

Teacher says ...

Your child will come home very tired. Big school is different to preschool. Forget everything that has to be done and take time out for hugs and cuddles when you first arrive home. Unwind together after a day apart. However, not all children will come home and want to chat about school. Some just want down time. This can be frustrating for parents, who may feel shut out. Be aware that this is quite common; it just depends on your child.

A parent says ...

Starting school is a special time in all our children's lives. I found it really useful to take my daughter to the school in the holidays. We then went to buy the stationery for 'big school'. It was very hard leaving my Number One. I felt more anxious than she did. There were tears, and that did make me feel worried. But the teachers were tremendous. They directed me to leave quietly, and distracted my daughter. Then they rang me five minutes later and told me she was now playing happily. I should have known!

Surviving the new regime

A child starting school has a big impact on family life – it is one of life's giant changes. Survive this new regime by getting involved, because school is as much about you as a parent as it is about your child as a learner.

DO ...

- ❖ go to the school's Orientation Day(s) so you and your child are familiar with the school buildings, bubblers, grounds, play equipment and routines before the 'big' day.
- ❖ get involved with your child's school from the start, in any way that your time and patience allows. Research shows clearly that kids do better at school if their parents are involved in some way.
- ❖ make sure your child has the same pencils, clothes and such equipment as the other children – and make sure they are all labelled and named.
- ❖ have 'child-friendly' equipment for them. Bags, lunchboxes, bottles, sandwich wraps – anything that they require must be manageable without your help. Lots of children bring to school lunchboxes and food items that are impossible for little fingers to open. This means the child requires great confidence to approach a teacher on duty to ask for help.
- ❖ try to meet the teacher, even briefly, in the first few weeks so that your child is not just an unknown face in that squirming, sniffling mass of uncivilised humanity. When you meet for the first time, simply introduce yourself, make the connection with your child and express your confidence that child and teacher will have a good year together.
- ❖ anticipate that the kids may be a little tired and teary after school for a week or two, or even a term or two. Don't keep asking them how it went and then explore the problems (if there are any). Instead, promote a positive outlook, ask for all the good news and project all the amazing things that will happen in the future.
- ❖ get them to bed on time!

❖ try to have good breakfasts – some kids are slower than others in the morning, but get a good routine and promote good vibes around the house. Get to know what they will eat, so you can help their bodies and brains cope with the busy mornings at school.

❖ make sure you are on time to collect her from school, for the first few weeks especially. If you can't, make sure you let the teacher or school know in advance – so they can prepare your child.

❖ be on the look-out for signs of stress – headaches, tears, school refusal, baby talk, crankiness, clinginess, poor sleeping, poor eating. Most kids will show some of these as they try to cope with a brand new world. But if the symptoms continue, or increase after a week or two, make sure your child keeps going to school, and arrange to meet the teacher to compare notes about how to make things happier.

❖ remember to take a break for yourself, too. Catch up and say hello to a few other parents in the same predicament. After all, some of these parents may soon become your new friends – or parents of your child's new friends.

DON'T ...

❖ sabotage success by threatening that your child will 'be in trouble if you do that at school'.

❖ condemn the first day to failure by sending her off with promises of learning to read and tell the time. Kids will take you literally; those who have no idea of time and can't read will expect to pick it all up on the first day, and may become very disappointed if they can't read to Mum when they get home.

❖ forget to let her practise the things she'll need to know to survive socially. If she hasn't had practice at preschool in how to cope with group toileting, how to unwrap her lunch, how to ask for help, how to get her shoes and socks off and on, then we can expect the dreaded 'T-thing' problems: Tears, Tummy-aches, Tiredness and Testiness.

❖ rush out and stock up on all the school gear in case you 'miss out'. Wait at least until you've seen what other children who go to the school are wearing, or until you have talked to a few seasoned parents. But do make sure they wear the 'common' uniform. Kids get self-conscious if they are seen to be outwardly different.

❖ ask general questions when she comes home, such as 'How did school go?' That's like someone asking you, 'How are you going?' or 'How did work go?' If you want real answers, ask specific questions: 'Who did you sit next to?', 'What story did your teacher read to you?' If the reply is, 'I just played', great – playing is your child's best way of learning about life.

How to minimise separation anxiety

Separation anxiety is usually associated with young babies who, at about the age of nine months, are mature enough to remember who's who and who's not. They might explore away from their parent for a few seconds but always check to make sure the parent is still there. Gradually, with time, with confidence and as other people develop a growing place in their lives, the anxiety settles down until, in adult life, it might only provoke a few pangs at Christmas and on Mother's Day. If, however, there has been some trauma that threatens their confidence, such as a stay in hospital, an illness, a parent who is overly anxious or dependent on the child, or if the child is just naturally anxious and insecure, then the battle can last much longer.

For these anxious kids, the transition to preschool or to school, or any real separation from the parent can become very threatening. It has nothing to do with loving the parent more than other kids love theirs, although a lot of parents mistakenly believe this, because it's nice to be needed.

Teacher says ...

I've always told parents of anxious kids to leave something behind so the child will know Mum will be back. One mother told her child she could take something from her bag to reassure her, so the child grabbed a tampon and raced around the room with that – much to the mirth of the staff and the embarrassment of Mum.

In addition, routine offers security. Children can often pick up on the routine of leaving, so have the same farewell catchphrase, e.g. 'Have a lovely day and I will see you when school finishes', followed by a kiss, then leave quickly. Children soon learn that these words mean parents are leaving and that they will return.

How you can help

* Make sure your children have plenty of contact with other adults so they learn to feel more confident with others. Try to get your partner, family or friends to take the kids to school and/or out somewhere so they don't become over-dependent.
* Build up little steps of independence. This might mean experience with playgroups, staying with other kids and adults while Mum does some shopping or visits the doctor, or staying with Grandma or another close relative or friend.
* Make the first separations brief, so your child becomes confident you'll come back.
* Make sure your child knows what to do in case you are late (who to sit with, etc.).

Part Two

Thriving as a learner

'The illiterate of the twenty-first century will not be those who
cannot read and write, but those who cannot learn,
unlearn, and re-learn.'

Alvin Toffler

I n Part Two we lift the lid
on learning. Let's think
of learning as if we are
planting a seed, helping it
take root, watching it grow
and then admiring the way it
flowers. You have read Part
One and you have planted
your most prized possession
– your child – in the fertile
soil of a school ground. He
is now in 'kindergarten' – which literally means 'garden of
children'. And the children *are* going to bloom – but not all
at the same time and not all in the same way.

In a garden, we plant and appreciate different
shrubs and flowers. This section looks at a new model of
learning, one that allows children to blossom at school. To
understand this model of learning, we have to appreciate
that there is no such thing as the 'perfect' learner. All kids
learn differently – at different speeds and in different ways.
In every classroom, we have what we call the 'learning
allsorts'. Once we understand these differences, we can
encourage and support our children in all their variety.

Education or learning?

'What are we doing to our kids? We have more benchmarks, more standardised basic skills tests, more objectives and pro- gress checks, but many kids still don't listen, don't care, don't respect authority. To them it's always everybody else's fault. What are we really teaching? It seems to me, and to virtually every other teacher I meet, that we've lost something, we're missing something. Parents know it too, but they blame the school. Somehow I think we've all got to get back to basics, and I mean something much deeper than "basic skills".'

Warwick, Year 6 teacher, New South Wales

This letter from Warwick struck a professional nerve within us. Some- thing *is* missing. Pupils may be smarter, but are we producing better kids, happier humans and more successful adults? Maybe we've been pushing skills to the detriment of real education; maybe we need to re-interpret the old '3Rs' as respect, responsibility and relationships – because that's what real education should promote and produce.

What's the difference?

It is true to say that the traditional 3Rs are still the engines that drive our education system – but we have to be careful, for the emphasis on them can also put many kids off learning. With the increase in children entering preschool, we are seeing formal education starting at a younger and younger age. This is great if you have a child ready to learn, but it can be the start of years of torment for those kids – mostly young boys – who are just not ready to be prodded along the treadmill of learning outcomes.

It is time we all started asking the big questions – What is learning? How do we help our schools get the best from our kids? How do we value individuals in a system that groups kids together in 12-month 'age cage', and then ploughs on relentlessly, adding ever-more content? If kids don't get it, they just get pushed along the cattle crush of educational standards: they are offered special classes to help them 'know' what they are 'meant' to know at the time they are 'meant' to know it. We risk crushing self-esteem underfoot as our kids march towards Year 12 and tertiary education at a cracking pace.

The key to successful education is to teach our children to be successful learners, taking into account their individual needs. Learning can't happen unless our kids are ready, able and engaged in the learning process. A sign on the steps of a very famous London school quotes Plutarch: 'A child's mind is a fire to be kindled, not a vessel to be filled'.

There are fundamental pieces in the jigsaw puzzle that are being overlooked. It's time we considered a new learning model.

The VAH model

We have developed a learning model which can provide that 'something' that is missing. Our model is based on children being equipped with the right Values, positive Attitudes, and good Habits. We call it the VAH model.

The petals on the flower of learning are our good **habits**, built on sound routines and practice. The stronger the habit, the better we will blossom as learners.

The slugs are our **bad attitudes**, which try to eat away at our positive focus.

The leaves are our **good attitudes**, which help us tackle new tasks.

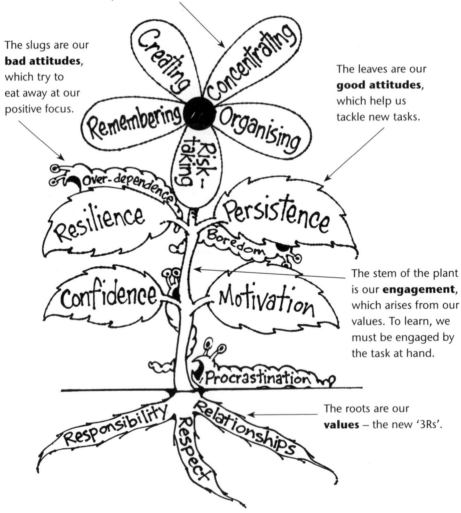

The stem of the plant is our **engagement**, which arises from our values. To learn, we must be engaged by the task at hand.

The roots are our **values** – the new '3Rs'.

Values

Values come from families, but are fertilised in schools. In a sense, schools are becoming the 'cathedrals' of the twenty-first century, and our kids are the trail-blazers of the information age. They *live* the IT revolution. Learners now have access to anything they need to know at the push of a button. This is new, exciting and very, very different to when we were kids. But there are other differences, too. We now have:

❖ bigger houses and greater wealth, but smaller backyards and smaller families
❖ more technology and multimedia, but less time together and less interaction
❖ more opportunities and easier access, but more restrictions and greater fears for our safety, and
❖ more material goods at cheaper prices, but more obesity and marketing to younger kids.

The result is we strive to keep our kids happy by giving them more, but we really give less. All these social changes mean that the values of today's Generation Y are different. If you ask your child about his values, you might be surprised when the Gameboy, computer, MP3 player or mobile phone is mentioned.

Values are much more than material goods, and they have a key role to play in learning. They are the springboard for the attitudes that a child demonstrates as a learner.

The new 3Rs for learning

The traditional 3Rs (reading, 'riting and 'rithmetic) may be fine for educating smart kids, but they are not adequate for growing smart learners. We'd like to propose some new 3Rs for learning:

1 respect
2 responsibility, and
3 relationships and social connections.

Respect

Any teacher will tell you that learners need to respect themselves, respect others (including the teacher!), respect property and respect the environment. It would be a great boost to children's chances of thriving at school if parents granted teachers unqualified respect from the start. Surely teachers have earned that right, having dedicated their professional lives to the important and challenging task of educating our children. Teachers, parents and kids all respecting each other – and working together – is the single most powerful value we can develop in a community of learners.

Responsibility

Kids these days have a strong sense of fairness. They are also very quick to assert their own rights. That's great, but what is often missing from the equation are the responsibilities that inevitably accompany the rights. Kids must take greater responsibility for their actions. And parents must understand that schools have to assert rules to ensure that all kids do act responsibly. Parents often have a different relationship with schools these days: in past generations, if a child came home complaining about something at school, parents would usually jump to the support of the school. These days, however, the reaction is often to question and doubt the school, and trust that our children are right. Taking this stance will very successfully erode the key nexus of kids, parents, teachers and school.

Relationships and social connections

The technological 'babysitters' that our kids are growing up with today are wonderfully good at entertaining: they give kids exactly what they want, when they want it, for as long as they want – and they don't answer back. You would think we should all be truly grateful for such technology, but we aren't. As a result of such technological generosity, our kids may be less capable of relating to others or forming the social connections that used to be common in childhood. We are now seeing more cases of social dysfunction and conduct disorder than ever before (see Appendix I for more information) – so much so that some schools have introduced social-skills programs to teach kids how to 'play' with each other. And the media nannies have also changed parents' views of the world: we are now anxious about letting our kids out – there are so many dangers. It seems much safer to stay inside the bedroom, connected by wire but disconnected socially.

Our 3Rs are basic. They are about *the whole child* – respect for adults, responsibility for themselves, and relationships with peers. How can parents promote these values? They're so basic, they're caught, not taught – just live them!

Attitudes

A true tale ... Brodie

Brodie was a boy with 'attitude'. He was capable of good work, enjoyed Harry Potter books, but just couldn't care. School was 'dumb', 'boring'. Brodie didn't do homework; he did as little in class as he could get away with and just lived for BMX. Dad was a mechanic who had hated his school days; he was now president of the local BMX club. Brodie was learning ... that school wasn't for him. The last time we heard from Brodie, he and Dad had split from Mum and were going around Australia in search of BMX glory.

Brodie had learned attitudes that made success at school very difficult.

Attitudes are like the leaves on a plant: they feed engagement, and stem from the values that are deep-rooted in all of us. The core values we highlight as the modern 3Rs – respect, responsibility and relationships (with social connections) – strengthen positive attitudes that are needed for learning. Attitudes are viewpoints: how we register something – be that positive, negative or neutral.

The switch-ons for learning – good attitudes

The following are positive attitudes that can promote successful learning:

❖ motivation
❖ confidence
❖ persistence, and
❖ resilience.

All kids have these attitudes. It's just that those who are thriving as learners in school use these attitudes in their approach to learning. They seem to have more of these qualities, and they use them more often.

Motivation

As children travel along the education pathway, they will need to become more independent. To thrive as a learner, to be engaged in the learning process, kids need to become motivated. It is clear that parents who push agendas are really asserting their own needs. Kids aren't stupid – they work it out. Sooner or later there will be a clash. If your child does not feel or acknowledge a 'need', he will get to an age and then rebel. We should motivate kids so that their drive comes from their own sense of need – their desire – not what we shovel onto them.

Top tips: what you can do

One way of motivating boys and girls hinges on Glasser's five basic needs – the basic need for survival plus the four psychological needs of belonging, power, freedom and fun.

Belonging increases via:
➡ time spent alone with Dad, Mum and friends
➡ team sport, clubs or groups (e.g. scouts, air cadets), and
➡ peer outings (excursions, mates over, trips).

Power increases via:
➡ cooking for oneself (and cleaning up!)
➡ doing jobs around the house – taking responsibility for some part of domestic life (e.g. pool, pets, room, lawn, etc.), and
➡ receiving and managing pocket money.

Freedom increases via:
➡ choices with outings, mates, party invitees
➡ selection of books to be borrowed from library
➡ timing for doing daily routines and jobs, and
➡ self-care of bodily hygiene (at primary ages).

Fun increases via:
➡ playing on the computer
➡ some form of indoor and outdoor entertainment
➡ physical activity with others, and
➡ roughhouse play, jokes and humour-sharing with parents.

Teacher says ...

Praise your child for effort, not intelligence: praise linking performance to a child's intelligence when tackling a task develops more negative consequences than praising a child for his effort. Children who are praised for 'being smart' come to view intelligence as fixed, something they can't change. Children praised for their effort and hard work come to see intelligence as something they can develop and improve.

Confidence

Confidence is a crucial attitude to have when it comes to learning. As adults, we forget what it is like to put your hand up in front of more than 20 other peers and guess a possible answer, to try something new, to compete against others in a race or a test. When was the last time we, as adults, had to stand up in front of our colleagues and give a speech ... and then get 'marked' for it? Confidence is a catalyst for expanding our knowledge and our achievements. Confidence is the attitude that allows us to extend our 'real world' by stretching the boundaries that limit us. To tackle anything new often means overcoming our fears, having a desire, and feeling that the result will outstrip the worries. Confidence increases our self-esteem, and self-esteem is needed to increase confidence. Self-esteem, mixed with our willingness to engage in a new task, fuels the ignition stage of learning anything new!

Social confidence

One key to unlocking the puzzle of getting kids to mix freely is to build social confidence. Social confidence comes from mixing children with others. Play-overs, sleep-overs, trips to uncles, aunts and grandparents, trips to play in the park, parties, and other functions that allow socialising are great for getting kids to interact.

Top tips: what you can do

If you feel powerless, you increase your anxiety, which leads to less confidence. However, if you focus on your strengths, trust in the passage of time, and project ideas forward, you will learn to cope with any situation. Children learn a lot from your modelling. If parents lack confidence or feel powerless and anxious, it is more than likely their children will, too.

➡ *Give praise and positive reinforcement*: encourage your child to take on challenges.

➡ *Be an active listener*: to your child, how you think of him as a person is highlighted by your interest in what he has to say and do. Listen carefully, paying full attention.

➡ *Be hard on the issue; easy on the child*: if you are disciplining your child, focus on the inappropriate action, not the person. Don't become too personal. This has a negative impact: your child will start to feel stupid, or a 'bad' person.

➡ *Don't build up preconceived ideas*: all children struggle with some subjects and concepts. By stating they are 'no good' just makes them believe it.

➡ *Laugh with your child*: humour is truly a wonderful device for making us all feel connected. It is also important for character development that kids do not take themselves too seriously.

➡ *Be prepared to say sorry*: when relationships do get a little frayed, don't be afraid to apologise. Consider another wise saying: 'Never let the sun go down on an argument'. Have a cuddle and make up.

Persistence

Persistence is the ability to maintain action regardless of your feelings. You push on, overcoming that desire to quit. Louis Pasteur stated: 'Let me tell you the secret that has led me to my goal: my strength lies solely in my tenacity.'

Children who lack persistence give up. There can be displays of despair and anger if they don't know an answer immediately. The catch-phrase is usually, 'I can't do this; it's too hard!' Some children just throw down any old answer: this can be work avoidance. Others have the misconception that finishing a sheet of questions in the fastest time indicates success. This is because adults emphasise the importance of finishing and getting the job done. 'Have you finished your homework, yet? Hurry up!' echo around kitchen tables globally.

Top tips: what you can do

➠ *Be clear about your support role*: too often parents step in to give a helping hand, but instead give the answer. This can lead to what psychologists term 'learned helplessness'. Always give strategies or clues; don't just give the answer. If you do have to give the answer, take your child through the steps needed – show how you worked it out. From an early age, when children are exploring and experimenting, don't get into the habit of making it easy for them; let them try, re-try and fail a bit, and come back to it later. You might be surprised to find they will return to it if you praise them for their effort.

➠ *Break down a task ('chunking')*: what seems a huge, complex problem is really just a lot of little tasks. If there is a large sheet of questions, colour them in groups of three, five or seven (these are the groups our working memory favours most). Encourage your child to tackle each group one at a time.

➠ *Use planning sheets and scaffolds*: overcome the fear of the dreaded blank page by using story plans, especially with boys, who may lack confidence in exploring or writing down thoughts. Get your child to focus on just the opening sentence, then the opening paragraph: once the ideas emerge, he will inevitably get carried away by his wonderful imagination.

➠ *Promote activities that are project-based*: lengthy projects, such as model-building or arts and crafts, require small steps and take extended periods of time to complete.

➠ *Expect your children to complete chores at home*: set out clear guidelines for chores your children have to complete. Maybe get them involved in identifying and selecting jobs, so they're more motivated to be involved. If they're seven or older, consider paying them for extra jobs so they earn some money and become more responsible around the house.

'Many of life's failures are people who did not realise how close they were to success when they gave up.'

Thomas Edison

Resilience

As much as we want our kids to be happy, things do go wrong at times. Just as happiness and excitement are great motivators for learning, feelings of anxiety, embarrassment and sadness are also key emotions for learning, too. For example, Jimmy Connors – the great tennis player – summed up his success by saying, 'I hate to lose more than I like to win'.

Resilient kids tend to be optimistic and confident. They don't just live the problem, but actively try to solve it; they are alert and not overly dependent on others.

What promotes resilience

* *Caring and supportive relationships* – where there is a role model or confidant(e) that children can trust.
* *Positive and high expectations* – by setting high expectations in a positive light, children learn to believe in themselves and in their future.
* *Opportunities for meaningful participation* – encourage your child's talents by creating opportunities to explore them.

Top tips: what you can do

➡ *Frame* the conflict or trouble by comparing it with hardships that others less fortunate have to deal with. This doesn't mean you downplay your child's concern or trouble; emphasise that resilient strategies are vital for life.
➡ *Project forward.* Acknowledge the pain and worry that he is currently feeling, but be positive by looking to the future, and highlight the valuable lessons he is learning.
➡ *If appropriate, highlight that he doesn't have the problem –* maybe the problem is not his, but belongs to the other person.

Discuss why the other person may have been hurt, and what may be done to fix things up.

➠ *Use humour to counteract feeling bad.* Try to see the funny side, turning worry on its head. This has to be done sensitively, and timing is everything.

➠ *Give unconditional love* – reinforce that he is loved and is okay, even when others tell him that he is not.

What erodes resilience

You are not helping if you are:

❖ always bailing children out, covering for them or protecting them from anything unpleasant or boring or tedious

❖ becoming involved too soon in their problems instead of letting them try to solve their own challenges

❖ speaking FOR the child (often or all the time)

❖ expecting children to act and respond like adults

❖ placing too much emphasis on academic and sporting skills, not encouraging interpersonal skills and compassion

❖ comparing your child with others: 'Why can't you be like ...?'

❖ running down authority figures in front of children

❖ either not setting or not enforcing guidelines or boundaries, or

❖ hiding your own struggles, disappointments, etc., from your kids, which makes them think bad things only happen to them.

A true tale ... the bright side

It is better to be optimistic. A father tries to pep up his sons. To the pessimistic one, he gives a gold watch; to the optimistic one, he gives a pad of dried horse dung. The pessimistic son said, 'Oh, yeah, where did this junk come from – Bali?' The optimistic son looked at his gift of dung and said, 'Wow, where's the horse?'

The switch-offs for learning – bad attitudes

If children are not engaged in good learning habits, they are switched off. This doesn't mean they are not learning; they are. They are learning *bad* habits – or reinforcing bad attitudes. We all have our switch-offs, so let's be open to them.

Switch-off	Possible cause	Cure
Frustration	Work too difficult, cutting into other interests, not the correct equipment, overtired.	Don't push the issue – allow cool-off time. Have the right equipment and wait until your child is motivated (remember, engagement is key to learning).
Impulsiveness	Excited, interested, or wants to complete the task as quickly as possible to get onto something new.	Consider using a timer. Lead into instructions by saying, 'There are three things I want you to do', so the child has to wait to hear all three. Break down the activity into 'fast' parts and 'patient' parts, to indicate speed.
Boredom	Similar to frustration – it is disengagement caused by a lack of interest.	Push through for the first 10 minutes, keep the child on task, 'chunk' information to help celebrate achievement. Emphasise effort.
Avoidance or procrastination	Unlike boredom, this usually has a negative reason beyond lack of interest – perhaps poor organisation, worry or stress.	Set out a good time plan. Set deadlines, and visually represent them. 'Chunk' down a big task into stages.
Intolerance	Intolerance usually comes from some bad attitudes and from a corrupted set of values.	Open up to different activities with different people. Model tolerance for learning new things as well as appreciating differences among people and cultures.

Switch-off	Possible cause	Cure
Distraction	Distraction can come from boredom, worry, poor class placement or a medical need. If there is consistent distraction, then consult a paediatrician or a clinical psychologist.	Have minimal items on the desk when a child is working. Make sure television and other distractions can't be heard or seen. Have a sibling participate in an activity as well.
Fearfulness	This is closely linked to risk-taking strategies. Fearfulness is an inner voice that is not feeling brave.	Chip away at the fear. If it is a fear of getting something wrong, focus on making mistakes as part of learning. Discuss people who have overcome great worries to achieve success. Don't show your own fears – be confident.
Over-dependence	This is very easy to promote, especially in younger children. Over-dependence means constant requests for help.	Instead of giving an answer, take the time to lead your child through a questioning process to discover a solution. Set chores to be completed – and have high expectations.
Perfectionism	This can lead learners to experience a stifling of creativity, task incompletion, frustration and procrastination.	See Part Three for lots of good advice.

Habits

Okay, so now our kids are connected in school – they are deep-rooted in the values of the school community and they are engaged: they love going to learn. They have positive attitudes and are thriving. Just as basic values underpin our attitudes, so those attitudes underpin our thinking habits, or 'habits of the mind'.

To flower, our kids need to develop specific habits of the mind. These habits are the tools of good learning ... and tools for having a good life. There are five key habits necessary to thrive as a learner:

1 organising
2 concentrating
3 remembering
4 creating, and
5 risk-taking.

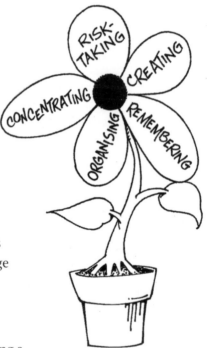

Imagine that these habits are the petals that shape our blossoming learner.

Just as there are negative attitudes that eat away at our learning potential, so too there are negative habits that we need to overcome. The negative habits that parents need to discourage are:

❖ over-criticising
❖ blaming others
❖ complaining without presenting a solution
❖ threatening, and
❖ lying.

Every one of us has these habits, but a thriving child overcomes them by learning how to be positive and improve as a learner.

Organising

Organisation is much more than just making your bed in the morning, but that's a start. Organising means putting things in order – so you know where they are. You can organise your thoughts, your time, your priorities and your possessions.

Top tips: What you can do

➠ *Model the behaviour*: children will do what they see their parents doing. If parents are organised, and if parents emphasise the importance of being organised, you are more likely to have organised children.

➠ *Establish consistent routines*: children love routines. From a young age, children find security in knowing there is an order and meaning associated with their environment. It is empowering for a child to take control of things, even if it is just by cleaning up! Organise a dedicated place for your children to complete homework, and try to have dedicated times, such as starting on the hour or half-hour. Have your child (with your help if required) empty his school bag every afternoon, placing any work or books (and the bag) in a specific location.

➠ *Set tasks that are appropriate to your child's ability*: this sounds like common sense, but setting tasks that are achievable, rather than unachievable tasks that cause stress, is vital. Don't set your children up for failure because your expectations are too great.

Teacher says ...

For some disorganised children, it is useful to have a separate pencil case left at school. Colour coding works well, too – have different coloured folders that are labelled for specific things (homework, reading, notes, etc.). Also, encourage your child to use different coloured highlighters on instructions or directions on sheets.

A parent says ... homework

I set a 20-minute egg timer for my children. That way, they focus on their homework for 20 minutes, then have a 10-minute break, when they can rest and have a glass of water. I always try to start homework at a specific time – on the hour, a quarter past, half past, or a quarter to. This helps to overcome procrastination.

Concentrating

Concentration helps link a chain of thought. There are two sources of concentration loss: internal distracters (when kids can't screen out irrelevant thoughts) and external distracters (from the environment, e.g. kids talking, other sounds, movements, etc.).

What usually happens is that we switch off when something doesn't turn our brains on. Remember – kids have to be engaged to learn!

Top tips: What you can do

➠ *Find your child's 'hotspot'.* A hotspot is an interest that can be used as a catalyst around which other learning is positioned.

➠ *Play concentration games* – and try to find games that suit a range of learning preferences (see also pages 68–69): if your children learn best through their eyes, convert boring things into images, diagrams, etc. If they learn best through their ears, convert information into rhymes and catchy tunes. If they learn by touch and feel, play an action game such as tic-tac-toe with chairs and people, or set out a grid and have a pathway through it that kids have to navigate from trial and error.

➠ *Give them an extended task,* like making a model aeroplane, or chores that require concentration to complete, such as gardening.

If you have a gut feeling something is wrong, have your child checked for any physical problem such as fatigue, poor hearing, ear infections, a thyroid problem or hearing loss. If that gets the all-clear, then ask for a psychological check either through the school counsellor or guidance officer, or with a private educational psychologist. This is to determine whether the problems are intellectual, emotional, social, or just bad habits that have formed over time.

A true tale ... Fred

Fred was blamed for being naughty when, in fact, he had a concentration problem that was out of his control. We looked closely at what we were expecting of Fred, and introduced a reward system that gave him a break of two minutes with his video game if he had worked well for 15 minutes.

As well, his teacher started a red/green system: a card with a red circle on one side and a green circle on the other was kept on the top left-hand corner of Fred's desk. When he lost concentration, his teacher flipped the card to red and moved it one space to the right, but no big fuss was made; when Fred worked hard, the card was flipped back to green and moved left, back a space. Fred's job was to keep that card to the left of the centre of his desk. If he did, rewards followed; if not, he had to miss out on some free time to catch up on work.

Part of the encouragement was that Fred was included in the process. If he did well, he would be allowed to keep something on his desk like the other kids had, but which had proved too much of a temptation before (e.g. ruler, pens and pencil sharpener).

Remembering

Learning is remembering. And learning is closely linked with understanding something. Unless new knowledge is hooked into existing brain networks, it will be forgotten. As learners, we can only hope to improve when we link what we have done, experienced or been taught to what we are going to do, or what we are thinking of doing. So how can we improve memory?

Focus when processing new information

As Dr Samuel Johnson (who created the first English dictionary in 1755) wrote, 'The true art of memory is the art of attention'.

Use mnemonics

Mnemonics are the strategies or tricks that people use for improving memory. These include:

* *Acronyms* – you form a word by using the first letter of each word you are trying to remember, e.g. 'FACE' (the notes in music).
* *Acrostics* – you create sentences in which every word starts with the first letter of the words you want to memorise, e.g. 'Every Good Boy Deserves Fruit' (notes in music).
* *Rhymes and Songs* – you make funny rhymes or songs that represent information, e.g. 'Thirty days hath September, April, June and November ...'.
* *Method of Loci* – this is an ancient Greek method that involves organisation, association and visual memory. You think of a route you commonly take, such as walking around your house. You then choose specific items you see on your walk along the chosen route, and select a number of items equal to the number of things you want to remember. Then you associate each of the things you want to learn, visually coding them against each item you remember along the route you mentally recall.
* *'Chunking'* – our short-term memory can hold around seven items. Chunking is where we group things, e.g. the phone number 94631993 can be grouped as 94 63 19 93 or 9463 1993.

❖ *Repetition* – saying something over and over again.
❖ *Use the other brain 'hemisphere'* – many students rely just on word/
auditory memory, what we call 'left-brain' learning. Converting
concepts to timelines, diagrams, story bubbles, etc. will help visual
learners to remember better.

Use external devices

These are the systems we use and develop to improve memory – such as
writing a key word on your hand, sticking a list to the fridge, etc.

Use a range of senses

We can associate new concepts with more than just visual, auditory or
kinaesthetic stimuli. Have a bunch of lavender or some other aroma to
associate with a concept you're trying to memorise. When you want to
recall the memory, take a sniff of the smell associated with the learning.

Consider using mind maps

Mind maps set out information on a page in a way that mimics how our
brain functions.

Creating

Being creative is considered the highest order of thinking. Without it, our thinking is stuck in simple recall. Memory is a great storage system, but thriving as a learner requires us to go beyond just knowing facts. We need to think, and thinking is much, much more than just recalling.

Dr Jamie McKenzie worries that children today have electronic shovels that cut and paste other people's ideas – they can *find*, but do they *think*? For example, many parents push their kids to learn the times tables by rote. A good Maths student in Year 3 can tell you that $6 \times 4 = 24$ straight up. But rephrase the question using an array as shown below, and his knowledge hits a hurdle. Learners who are still mastering a higher-order understanding of Maths strategies go back to counting the squares one by one.

What this shows is that the student does not have a true understanding of what a 'table' really is. The child cannot apply this knowledge.

To help, try writing numbers on the grid (in this case, 1 to 24) to show that each square is represented by a number, and that the grid is a 'table' of numbers. For kids who do master this, try giving them irregular rectangle shapes – this will encourage them to break tables into parts, and is a great lead into questions about area.

How to promote creativity and higher-order thinking skills

▶ Allow for individuality to shine – celebrate differences.

▶ Question children to get them to consider other possibilities.

▶ Use humour to develop fantastic ideas that go off on a tangent and seem really silly.

▶ Allow for the messy exploration of new ideas without getting cross.

▶ Build social networks with different people.

▶ Be enthusiastic about learning new things and thinking in different ways.

▶ Offer the space and time for being creative – with resources that allow for experimentation.

▶ Challenge assumptions.

▶ Encourage sensible risk-taking, and allow for mistakes to be seen as fundamental stages in learning.

▶ Delay gratification – don't jump in to praise, consider other possibilities. At times, let your child struggle with a topic.

▶ Stimulate more lateral thinking by asking 'What if … ?' questions.

▶ Avoid criticism that shames or blames children when they are experimenting through trial and error.

Teacher says … paralysis through analysis

Paralysis through analysis can happen to any learner. Consider a golf game. The coach tells you to pull in your elbows, bend the knees, keep your eye on the ball, roll around as if on a chair, grip the club properly. Your brain starts to focus on so many little details that it freezes, producing a worse effort. With children, just tackle a few matters at a time; don't try to analyse or correct everything in one go. Enjoyment is the key to repeated effort.

Risk-taking

Sensible risk-taking is an important part of thriving as a learner because it helps our kids test out theories ... and their luck. It also makes them appreciate truly dangerous risks. Our concern is that many parents are trying to shelter their children from all risks because there is some inherent danger in being a child.

Encourage your child to take responsible risks. Risk-taking builds confidence. If learning takes us outside our comfort zone, it's necessary to overcome attitudes that want to reduce risk. There are some key steps in this process:

❖ *Clarify*. Consider what is the benefit – what do you get from taking the risk? Is the reward worth it? What is the worst thing that could happen? Can you live with that?

❖ *Plan*. Have an action plan that includes all the steps and the deadlines. Consider who can help. Think about how smart risk-takers would tackle a situation. What do you need to do? What are the obstacles, and can you get motivated to tackle them?

❖ *Reflect*. What have you learnt from past situations? What strategies have you developed that can support you in this situation?

❖ *Role-play*. Rehearse the situation. Go over it in your mind to practise the challenge. Use positive self-talk. Visualise what you will do.

❖ *Build on your successes*. The more you involve yourself in responsible risk-taking, the easier it gets. Take small risks and build on them. Imagine you are exercising a muscle – the more training you do, the stronger it becomes.

❖ *Celebrate and evaluate*. When you do overcome fear of a risk, take the time to celebrate and reward yourself. Think about what worked and what didn't, so you can prepare yourself for more responsible risks in the future.

❖ *Share memories* of your own mistakes to alleviate the worry children feel about making a mistake. Talking about the fear of making mistakes with your children reduces the worry.

Note: It is very rare to find a child who will attempt calculated risks in a home where parents never leave their own comfort zones or enjoy a challenge.

Teacher says ...

The fear of making mistakes, taking risks and looking foolish is one of the strongest roadblocks to developing self-esteem and resilience. Children are often vulnerable to feelings of defeat and are likely to retreat from tasks that may lead to failure. Children and adults often look at risk-taking in different ways: a child looks at risks in terms of what may be gained; a parent looks at risks in terms of what may be lost!

To risk is to live

The following anonymous poem is a reminder that risk is an essential part of life.

To laugh is to risk appearing the fool.
To weep is to risk appearing sentimental.
To reach out is to risk involvement.
To expose feelings is to risk exposing your true self.
To place your ideas and dreams before the crowd is to risk their
   love.
To love is to risk not being loved in return.
To live is to risk dying.
To hope is to risk despair.
To try is to risk failure.
But the greatest hazard in life is to risk nothing.
The one who risks nothing does nothing and has nothing – and
   finally *is* nothing.
He may avoid suffering and sorrow
But he simply cannot learn, feel, change, grow or love.
Chained by this certitude, he is a slave; he has forfeited freedom.
Only one who risks is free!

The many types of intelligence

Going through school often leads to parents worrying whether their kids are 'intelligent' – it can even become a competition, with parents wanting their kids to be smarter. But 'intelligence' is being too narrowly defined, too closely linked with IQ.

Intelligence is much more than just academic knowledge. Professor Howard Gardiner suggests that there are many types of intelligence: he outlined seven – and then later changed it to eight. Eight? Were people getting smarter? No, just greener: the eighth is 'naturalistic intelligence' (i.e. being 'nature-smart').

The eight are:

1 linguistic intelligence (good with words)
2 logical mathematical intelligence (good with numbers and reasoning)
3 spatial intelligence ('picture-smart')
4 bodily kinaesthetic intelligence ('body-smart')
5 musical intelligence (good at music)
6 interpersonal intelligence (good at meeting and befriending people)
7 intrapersonal intelligence (good at understanding oneself), and
8 naturalistic intelligence ('nature-smart').

The benefit of this approach is that it allows us to see all our kids as having special strengths. It gives parents a framework to celebrate differences in learners.

There is also another aspect of intelligence that is crucial to happiness and achieving potential: 'emotional intelligence' (EI). People with high EI are capable of understanding others, are more successful in relationships, and have greater self-control, which makes for a more positive outlook.

Furthermore, Thomas Friedman, in his book *The World is Flat*, highlights, via the equation CQ + PQ > IQ, that curiosity (CQ) and passion (PQ) are far more important than intelligence (IQ) for successful learning. So it's all relative.

Gardiner's theory of multiple intelligences

The 'learning allsorts'

We take the view that all children have talents, and have more intelligence in some areas than others. We are yet to find the 'perfect' child. If we want kids to work on their weaknesses, they must first find their strengths so they feel they are worthwhile people with some areas to improve. It's hard to be motivated to improve if you feel that you're 'dumb' or an academic disgrace to the family. Let's celebrate differences. Let's celebrate the 'learning allsorts'.

'Slow' learners

For kids who can't keep up, school looms as a sentence of ten years' hard labour, with a bit of time off if they are expelled for bad behaviour. They can become very resentful and anti-school. It is like battling every day for ten years only to be told you are a failure – but to keep on trying anyway. Slow learners are often a little below the average age in a classroom.

School reports are likely to mention phrases such as 'having difficulty', 'poor concentration' or even 'tries hard'. These terms may mean that schoolwork is a real struggle and that action needs to be taken quickly.

How to help

- ❖ Check with the teacher to see if progress is below average – and don't be put off by the 'they'll catch up' line.
- ❖ If the teacher is concerned, ask for an intellectual assessment by the school counsellor or local psychologist – it's not just an IQ test, it's the equivalent of a medical overhaul to see how your child's brain is ticking and how best to tailor a program to suit his learning profile.
- ❖ On the basis of that assessment, ask the school for a two-way plan of action that will not only help the child's weaknesses but also find his strengths, so he need never feel a total failure.
- ❖ On the home front, that plan of action must not be an extra dose of schoolwork, although a tutor can often work wonders with skills and morale. Include opportunities to achieve in areas in which your child shows flair. Each child is unique, and each child brings to the family some talents that can be the core of his self-worth.
- ❖ Kids can be cruel to anyone who is different or weaker, so be prepared for some teasing and name-calling (e.g. 'spaz', 'idiot', 'drop-kick'). Help with some tease-tossing tactics (see our section on bullying in Part Four) and mention the problem to the teacher.
- ❖ Teaching slow learners often requires paying more attention to the practical side of learning, teaching with everyday examples and materials, handling abstract work in short sessions, and adjusting learning goals so they are within reach.

A true tale ... Karen

Karen was the eldest of three girls. As she grew older, her sisters were able to do her work better than she could. When she asked her mum how to spell a word, her sisters always chimed in because they wanted everyone to know how clever they were. Karen's parents changed the homework routine so that Karen did her homework in private.

But Karen knew she was falling further and further behind. By Year 6 she hated school. The breakthrough came at high school. Karen found new friends, took different subjects, and was in a class with kids of her own ability. Her parents also discovered she was becoming a talented young chef. Her sisters enjoyed her new culinary skills, and this won their respect. There was no more competition because the kids were now running different races.

Gifted learners

In the school business, there is a distinction made between a 'gift' and a 'talent'. Generally, a 'gift' is a natural disposition, while a 'talent' is something that is drilled or trained. Gifts can go undeveloped if not nurtured properly. And there is a difference between 'bright' children and 'gifted' children (see the table below).

Parents like to think of giftedness as divine proof of genetic genius. But gifted learners are not any happier than the average child, they don't get better jobs, and they don't necessarily earn more money.

Bright	Gifted
Knows the answers	Asks the questions
Is interested in things	Is a highly curious explorer
Is focused and attentive	Is highly mentally and physically involved
Likes words	Uses complex, often unusual, vocabulary
Has good ideas	Has flamboyant, silly ideas
Works 'hard'	Mucks around yet tests well
Answers the questions	Discusses in detail, elaborates
Listens with interest	Shows strong feelings and opinions
Learns with ease	Knows already
Needs six–eight repetitions for mastery	Mastery after one or two repetitions
Understands ideas	Develops abstract ideas
Enjoys peers	Prefers adult company
Grasps the meaning	Explores implications
Completes assignments	Starts projects
Copies accurately	Creates new designs
Enjoys school	Enjoys learning
Adept at memorising	An inventor
A technician	A great guesser
Enjoys simple, clear logic	Thrives on complexity
Is pleased with own learning	Is highly self-critical

Although parents like having gifted kids, it is the bright kids who usually fit in better and make the top students. Gifted kids often have a hard row to hoe in life and need lots of special understanding. There is also a tendency for many parents (and some teachers) to equate superior academic performance with giftedness. All children are gifts and all children have gifts.

It's also about time we recognised and respected other gifted learners in areas such as mathematics, music, art, performing arts, sport and social intelligence. There are also some myths about giftedness that need closer scrutiny:

❖ Far from being guaranteed academic success, *gifted children are probably the most underachieving of all school populations.*

❖ Gifted children do not need more 'teaching', but the reverse – more opportunities to learn. *Gifted students are capable of learning with relatively little teaching.*

❖ Emotional intelligence, resilience, confidence, social skills and *involvement in outside-school activities are much better predictors of real-world success than are high IQ scores or grades.*

Teacher says ...

Almost every teacher we surveyed expressed the same opinion: if you feel your child is gifted, talk to the teacher for an objective opinion and, if appropriate, extension work (i.e. different work, not more of the same) can easily be provided. Many teachers will compact their teaching, taking out any repetition of topics so that gifted children can be extended with more details or higher-order concepts.

Dealing with gifted learners

- Don't compare your gifted child with other children. All children are unique and special in their own way, and need to focus on their own abilities, not how they do compared to others.
- Don't expect your gifted child to fulfil all of your own unachieved aspirations.
- Children don't have to be 'gainfully' employed every waking moment. There should be time for daydreaming, clowning around, watching TV, reading comics, playing on the computer and lying on an unmade bed to contemplate the ceiling.
- All kids need exposure to libraries, art galleries, museums and historical places, but regular visits by a gifted child ensure these places become user-friendly for the child. These kids become free to explore the world through books, nature, science, prehistoric monsters, or anything else that takes their interest, and it all enhances their hunger for knowledge and skills.
- Read biographies and introduce your child to people who have succeeded by persisting in the face of adversity. Show respect for hard work as well as innate ability. Praise your child for effort and trying, for wonderful things done, even though they may not have worked out as hoped. Enquiring minds must take intellectual risks, and this needs encouragement and support. Demonstrate the importance of effort in your own life and take some intellectual risks yourself!
- Assume that these kids intend to do the right thing, especially when questions of authority arise. Don't become defensive just because their logic challenges power-based management. Listening to their point of view doesn't mean you have to agree.
- Gifted kids are sometimes impatient with conventions of politeness and manners, but they can be helped to rationally see the social advantages of courtesy and how it relates to respect for others.

- It's harder for schools to cater totally for gifted kids, so forge links with groups or teams that can cater to their special interests. An Internet search will reveal associations that run camps, weekend workshops and information nights, with lots of ideas to help parents of gifted kids.
- Mentoring links up the child with a knowledgeable other person – an adult or an older child – who can inspire, guide, role-model and enhance the child's own current expertise. It may be arranged through the child's school, but any program should not be too structured and should be allowed to develop naturally. A mentor needs to be chosen carefully.

Above all, enjoy your gifted child. Gifted children are curious, enthusiastic, excited about new things and able to communicate at a sophisticated level early! Some of this is likely to rub off on all those lucky enough to know and love a gifted child.

'Lazy' learners

No kids are more frustrating to teach or to help than 'lazy' learners. Sometimes it seems that their pens are too heavy to lift, their heads too heavy to hold up, or that life is just too heavy altogether! But laziness is often the *result* of a problem, not the cause.

How to help

❖ Find out where the child is being lazy – if it is at school, try to find out why; if it is at home, try to discover the causes there; but if it is all the time, consult a doctor. A full medical check can reveal problems such as allergies, glandular fever, low-grade infections, chronic fatigue, thyroid problems, diabetes, anaemia, or any other ailment that may be causing the lack of energy.

❖ High-achievement-orientated homes can also be a factor. 'Laziness' is a highly successful countermove against parents who expect too much. Children who can't out-power powerful parents will often use passive resistance. That way no-one can ever accuse them of answering back, being rude or showing temper. The hidden aim is to make their parents feel as bad as they do. Passive resisters need parents to rethink their approach and 'lighten up', so a friendlier and more cooperative relationship can blossom.

Many 'lazy' learners just feel like failures – like Davo (see the next page)!

A true tale ... Davo

Twelve-year-old Davo walked gawkily into my clinic, slumped down into a chair and, with his head down, made sure he avoided eye contact. The note from his father said, 'The kid is bone idle', so we started to investigate.

Actually, Davo was very talented: he had a brilliant vocabulary, incredible comprehension, was terrific at Maths and, in fact, fell into the top 1 percent of the students. The problem was that Davo wasn't very good at practical skills. His father, on the other hand, was a top electrician, big on 'right-brain' talent and very practical. He wanted Davo to go into the family business, but all Davo wanted to do was read, analyse and study, all 'left-brain' activities.

His father was bitterly disappointed in Davo, and the boy knew it. He had failed the 'family fitness test'. He wasn't lazy, just lonely.

Once his father recognised the reasons for the rift, his opposition to Davo diminished overnight and he started to accept the boy as he was, not as he had wanted him to be.

Teacher says ...

My son was lazy. I think it was because I was so busy I'd end up doing things for him, to get them done. When I realised I was making him lazy, I decided to put as much effort in as he did. If he hadn't done much to help out on his chores, I'd just not have time to help him with his homework or making anything special for dinner. I remember one time he was particularly offended: I had had to put up with his half-baked efforts, so I half-baked his dinner and said, 'Oh, it'll do, son'.

Perfectionists

Perfectionists are made in heaven, often moulded in a fussy home, and rounded off at school, but they are hard to live with – particularly for the person hiding inside the perfectionist. They must have everything right, will refuse to hand work in if there is a single error, will avoid anything that they can't accomplish perfectly, are critical of mistakes in themselves and others, never know when enough is enough, and spend hours on homework and assignments. Teachers often see perfectionists as really good kids, but they don't know the hell these kids cause at home.

How to help

❖ Have a conference with the teacher and agree to reward effort, imperfect and incomplete work only (don't worry about standards slipping, these kids provide their own pressure). For instance, see if they can be strong enough to get work wrong and not let it bother them, or strong enough to stop doing something they haven't quite finished and not worry about it.

❖ Encourage messy play, getting dirty, water play, rhythm, playing with pets ... anything to get their bodily defences down, as many of these kids are fearful of messy or free-for-all play.

❖ Be aware of how you use praise. Parental pride in a toddler's talent can lead to extravagant praise from a parent and the mistaken belief by the child that he should be able to do anything. Make sure you always:
  - praise action, not ego
  - praise effort, not just success
  - praise ability to handle failure as much as success, and
  - praise sharing, waiting, the ability to handle being second best, and other social skills vital for a happy childhood.

❖ Write out two permission notes for your child:

  1 I, _____ hereby give myself permission to be good at

  _____

  Signed _____ Date _____

2 I, _____ hereby give myself permission not to be so
good at _____
Signed _____ Date _____

❖ Examine your own behaviour. Do you highlight performance success
or enjoyment? Are you overcritical of your own performance? Do
you do too much for the children, implying that they can't do it for
themselves? Are you intolerant of their failures? Are you trying to
raise the perfect kid? Continually model, even if it hurts, that it is
okay to make mistakes, and happily accept the mistakes of others.
In other words, learn to go easy on yourself if you want the kids
to do likewise! *Many of the perfectionists we see in the classroom come
from homes where there is at least one parent who is totally obsessed with
cleanliness and fastidiousness around the house.* Perfectionism is not an
easy trait to live with; what many parents and teachers don't realise
is that it is a form of OCD (obsessive-compulsive disorder), which
can be very debilitating. (See Appendix I for more on OCD.)

❖ Perfectionism is an attitude, not an achievement, so use imaginary
characters or true stories about kids who have had to confront
similar problems and how they dealt with them.

Stressed learners

Stress has become the buzzword of the decade, describing the sense of overload that adults feel as they try to cope in a world on overload. Yet for some reason we treat stress as a purely adult problem, unaware that children are even more vulnerable, with less maturity to handle it all. But an interesting thing about stress is that it's a response to how we see things that depends not on fact but on feeling – it's due to how we perceive a problem.

Parents often miscalculate and misunderstand what is stressful to kids. For example, parents rate the birth of a new sibling as much more stressful to the other children than children rate it; children rate parental conflict much higher than adults do.

Top stressors for children

- parental divorce or separation
- repeating a year at school (especially for upper-primary or high-school students)
- wetting pants in class
- being suspected of lying
- receiving a poor report card
- being ridiculed in class
- academic failure
- social failure: not selected in a sporting team, not invited to parties, not invited to sit next to someone in class, etc.
- family failure: not matching up to brighter or faster school mates or siblings
- chronic illness, depression or conflict in the family
- conflict with a teacher, or getting in trouble for poor work or poor behaviour, and
- financial failure: not having enough money to go on school excursions, or to concerts, to have the same shoes as their friends, to buy food from the canteen, etc.

Identifying signs of stress

Parents sometimes find it difficult to identify a child under stress until the stress is quite serious – extreme acting-out or violence, suicidal ideation or self-harm. Below is a checklist for identifying stress – there may be cause for concern if your child presents with more than seven of these factors, or if one or two are quite extreme:

- ❖ sleeping late (even on weekends) or insomnia
- ❖ avoiding school
- ❖ fighting with siblings and friends
- ❖ displaying hostility to teachers and other adults
- ❖ general irritability and sensitivity to people and the environment
- ❖ complaints of physical illness (stomach aches, headaches)
- ❖ onset of bed-wetting or soiling
- ❖ nightmares
- ❖ increase in clumsiness and accidents
- ❖ trembling, nervous tics (twitches)
- ❖ teeth-grinding
- ❖ prolonged loss of appetite
- ❖ stuttering, and
- ❖ repeated movements: rocking, head-banging.

If you have the feeling that many of these symptoms resemble those children with defiant, aggressive and hostile behaviour ('naughty kids') rather than 'stressed kids', in a sense you'd be right – because many of the kids suffering stress are misdiagnosed as 'naughty'. Far too often, parents, teachers and health professionals treat the symptoms of the stressed child by targeting the disruptive behaviour rather than the cause.

Managing those stress levels

❖ From an early age, introduce novelty and new experiences often – this helps kids learn how to cope with change. Go to new cinemas, playgrounds, visit different friends, and involve the kids in some group such as mothers' groups, play groups, or later in more formal groups such as Cubs or Brownies, where excursions and new experiences are regular occurrences. Encourage the kids to accept change comfortably.

❖ In their schoolwork, look for improvement rather than perfection, and effort rather than success. Children soon learn it is difficult to be 'the best' at anything – there is always another child who is faster, stronger, smarter or better. Praising the child who tries his best is the surest way to ensure self-esteem can be maintained, regardless of performance levels.

❖ Help them find the sports, activities and hobbies they enjoy. That way they won't write themselves off as inadequate misfits if they struggle in some areas of schoolwork. What's more, if they run into trouble in one area (e.g. a sporting injury), they have other areas to fill the gap.

❖ Provide good models of behaviour – if *you* aren't coping with stress, how do you expect the kids to manage? Show your children that any stress can be dealt with in a constructive way – show them how to be problem-solvers, not just problem-livers. You won't only help yourself, you'll help your child, too.

❖ Create special down-time, cuddle time and play time so the whole family can relax. In a busy world, this time won't happen unless we treat it as a sacred priority. Switch off the television and play some quiet relaxing music, burn oils, play a board game, draw, cook together, massage – whatever makes the family feel good.

❖ Try to work out what the stressor in the child's life may be. For younger kids, this may mean keeping notes on when and where it's at its worst. For older kids, you can set up a 'grouch list' of everything that makes them feel 'yucky', and they can give each one a rating out of ten. Remember, if you can identify what has made your child stressed, then you're halfway to solving the problem.

Stress is simply a part of life for every individual – wherever they are, whatever they do and whatever age they are. Our job as parents is to help kids find ways to handle it so they can face life confidently, comfortable in their own coping system.

Teacher says...

A surprising number of teachers we surveyed commented that problems with organisation and time management were the big stressors for the children in their class. Help kids with those aspects and we may have better-coping kids.

Learning preference

A crucial question that many people forget to ask is, 'Do you know how you learn?' Knowing *how* you learn can greatly improve your ability *to* learn. In education circles this is termed 'metacognition'.

The ancient Greeks were probably the first to realise that people learn differently. Teachers are aware that many kids have a preference for certain methods of learning over others. These 'dispositions' we refer to as 'learning styles'. One of the first things teachers and parents should do to help a child 'learn' is to be aware that kids learn differently – and have different preferences.

There are probably as many ways to teach as there are to learn. By knowing that people do not all see the world in the same way, we can start to tailor our teaching to suit individual learning styles. In teaching terms, this is called 'differentiation'.

The VAK (Visual Aural Kinaesthetic) model

The VAK model is a framework teachers use to meet the different learning styles prevalent in classrooms. It uses the three major sensory receivers – visual (seeing), aural (listening), and kinaesthetic (doing or moving). Learners have a preference for receiving information using a dominant sense. For modern kids living in a world of multimedia and colour, this is most typically visual.

As children progress through school, the way we relay information changes from one dominant aspect to another. For example, preschoolers prefer kinaesthetic – lots of movement and activities. In primary school, the focus is more on visual learning, with presentations involving Power-point, lots of colours, illustrations and graphics. In high school and beyond, learning becomes more aural, with lectures and discussions.

It is important to point out that the VAK model requires us to identify a *preference* for a sense. And while *all* learners will use *all* their senses, we all have one that is dominant over the others. Luckily for children born in the new millennia, the burgeoning world of multimedia technology greatly enhances learning opportunities that benefit all three senses.

To help you identify your child's preference, see which of the following descriptions best suits him.

Visual learners are fine-tuned to information displayed in handouts, graphs and diagrams. They love all types of artwork – photos, cartoons, picture cues – as well as colours, shapes and visually varied formats. As most children are visual learners, playing to their strengths in the classroom is an effective way to teach.

Auditory learners like listening, which means they can do really well in most classrooms. They love to learn by using poems, riddles, tongue-twisters and jokes. While not so good with flashcards, they prefer to absorb information via the radio, tapes, podcasts and so on. These are the kids who can memorise commercials and entertain others with their impersonations.

Kinaesthetic learners love to be active – they thrive on a tactile, 'hands-on' approach. They usually excel at sport and at experiments that require physical involvement. However, their interest in their immediate surroundings can distract them from the task at hand. They love to be involved in drama and role-plays, gardening and making projects, and they will pull something apart just to see how it works. But beware: they are not always able to put it back together again!

The value of understanding the VAK model

The VAK model underlies the fact that information enters our brain via our senses. This can open our minds to begin considering *how* we learn, and how we can optimise our learning potential. Using a range of different stimuli strengthens our learning by passing the information into our memory for later recall.

Part Three

Thriving in the classroom

The essential areas of learning

'What we want to see is the child in pursuit of knowledge, not knowledge in pursuit of the child.'

George Bernard Shaw

It's a funny thing, education. It was introduced to help children learn about life, but we take them out of life, put them behind four walls with little windows and big fences, and proceed to tell them about life! And if they can't keep up, we say, 'Catch up'. But catch up with what? Is it really a race?

Classrooms are little boxes – which focus attention on the essential areas of learning, called the traditional 3Rs. Thriving in the classroom will focus on what we call English and Maths – what many believe to be the 'serious' subjects. We will give you some advice and some strategies, and give your kids some hope. But thriving as a learner is different from thriving in the classroom: the latter is about following a system, following routines and falling into line.

This Part looks at supporting our kids as they focus on reading, 'riting and 'rithmetic.

Note: Please read Part Two before Part Three.

Understanding reading

Think back to when you were a child – how did you learn to read? For some, it just seems to come naturally – we all know of kids who jump three reading levels in two months. Maybe the talent for reading is congenital, passed down from our parents and grandparents.

But go back to our section on learning, and we all should be worried. Education is becoming more and more formalised at an ever-younger age. It could be said that preschool nurseries are now the early years of 'big school'. As a result, some kids aren't ready. Reading, instead of being fun, becomes a chore – an unattainable one for some. We are excluding many boys from success because they are disengaged before they even have their motor running. And many of us now have an expectation that our kids will be reading *Harry Potter* in Year 2. We want to consider the important issue of readiness, not 'readingness'.

How does reading happen?

Reading requires a lot of energy and concentration. It involves all of these steps:

❖ focus on the printed marks on a page (letters and words)
❖ control of eye movement across the page
❖ awareness of how letters sound
❖ knowledge of words and grammar – how words are put together to make meaning
❖ visualising images and ideas
❖ linking new ideas to ones you already know, and
❖ storing ideas in your memory so they can be easily recalled.

A whole-word (visual) or a phonic (auditory) approach?

It is clear that a balanced approach – harmony between whole words and phonetic strategies – is best for developing good readers. Children need to gain strategies but they must also retain interest. 'Drill and Kill' is not conducive to enjoyment. Learning to read must remain fun and exciting.

When children reach a level of fluency where they can recognise a word automatically, they can spend their mental energy understanding what the word means – by itself and with other words.

For example, by the time children have become adult readers, the decoding stage is no longer a necessity. Consider the following passage:

> Aoccdrnig to a rscheearch at an Elingsh uinervtisy, it deosn't mttaer in what order the ltteers in a word are, the olny iprmoaetnt thing is that the frist and lsat ltteer are in the rghit pclae. The rset can be a total mses and uou can still raed it wouthit porbelm. This is bcuseae we do not raed ervey lteter by itslef but the word as a wlohe.

As we develop our reading skills, we move away from having to phonetically decode every letter sound and digraph to a whole-word awareness. Children progress from 'learning to read' to 'reading to learn'.

A true tale ... Kathryn

Kathryn was going crazy over her schools' efforts to help her to read. One school used the whole-word method, but Mum couldn't handle it – it wasn't real reading – so she swapped schools for Kathryn. The new school taught phonics, but Kathryn couldn't handle it, so they hired a whiz-bang, teach-your-child-to-read-everything-overnight (except the fine print!) book, and that failed. Now we had not just a remedial reader, we had a reluctant reader and a bitter parent. Learning to read a book is like learning to ride a bike: you don't analyse every part first, you climb aboard, have fun, enjoy the freedom, follow the rules, and have someone friendly around to pick you up if you fall or fail.

Kids generally take to phonics around age six or seven. Whole-word patterns tend to use the right brain, and phonic sounds tend to use the left, so a good reading program employs both strategies. Make reading for pleasure fun: use plenty of rhyme, rhythm and repetition, lots of pictures to talk about, and rich fantasy to think about.

The '3P' reading strategy

A good strategy for reading is 'Pause, Prompt, Praise' – or '3P'.

Pause

On finding an unknown word, give your child time to work it out.

Prompt

❖ Try again – go back to the beginning of the sentence or read on to the end of the sentence to encourage the use of context cues.

❖ Ask the child to look for a picture cue (do not cover up the pictures).

❖ Ask the child to look at the first letter – predict what the word may be.

❖ Ask the child to predict some vocabulary and grammar points, e.g. 'I s.... well last night' is 'I slept well last night'.

❖ Encourage your child to break words down – 'inside' becomes 'in' and 'side'. Point out endings such as '-ing' on known words, e.g. 'going'.

❖ Encourage the child to sound the word out – sounding is a useful tool in reading, but should not be overused. Do not make your child sound out every word.

❖ Sound a word out for your child.

❖ If necessary, tell your child the word, especially those with no picture cues such as 'where', 'here', 'they', etc.

❖ Discuss the meaning of the word.

❖ When reading a harder book, take turns to read a page or a sentence each.

❖ If your child is struggling with a book, give her cues when discussing the picture about the text, e.g. 'That swing looks like fun' (there is a picture of a swing on the page).

Praise

❖ Be positive – getting your child to want to read is half the battle.

❖ Even if mistakes are made, praise your child's efforts.

❖ Reading should be FUN!

❖ If you are raising your voice in anger or frustration – forcing your child to read – you are breeding reading resistance! Reluctant readers are developed, not born.

❖ Even though your child may be bringing home books from school, continue to read other books and stories to her.

Age-appropriate reading strategies

Toddlers

❖ Let toddlers 'read' their favourite books by themselves, and comment positively on their achievements. It doesn't matter if you read their favourites over and over again.

❖ When reading, pause before a familiar word and let the child say it. This works best with rhymes and repetitions.

❖ Read about things you are doing with your toddler – signs, pamphlets, directions, maps – so you model reading as a part of everyday life.

Preschoolers

❖ Add new books to your child's library as birthday presents and special gifts – but keep reading old favourites. Your child may now know the favourites by heart – this is an important step in learning about reading.

❖ Take your child to the library regularly to borrow books.

❖ Take your child shopping, and continue highlighting coupons, signs, directions, etc.

❖ Let your children join in cooking as you follow a recipe.

❖ Take books on long trips to encourage reading for enjoyment.

School-age children

Following are some ideas, but please take care: we would hate to think these ideas may lead parents to saturate their youngsters with all these strategies. As has been mentioned – and needs to be stated firmly again – forcing a child to read promotes reading resistance, not improvement.

❖ *Use the 'neurological impress' method* – read along with the kids so you are saying and pointing to the words while they try to say as many as they can with you. When you've read a paragraph or an easy page, go back and count how many words they got right this time.

- ❖ *Use 'echo' reading* – you read a line and the child reads this after you. This helps with expression and punctuation.
- ❖ *Use the 'paragraph-shrinking' method* – you read a paragraph and then shrink the main ideas down to no more than ten words (i.e. summarise it). The child then reads the second paragraph and does the same thing – this helps kids to glean the main concepts in what they're reading.
- ❖ *Have fun with the 'nudge nudge' method* – you begin reading and stop at a word, then nudge the child, who commences reading and who, in turn, nudges you back when she wants you to resume.
- ❖ *Embrace technology*! If you have a child who loves watching television or movies, turn on the teletext (subtitles in English). This is a great way to promote reading, and can save a lot of stress.
- ❖ *Build confidence.* Choose books that a child can read with 95+ percent accuracy. This level will ensure good fluency, accuracy and interest. Reading sessions should be no longer than 10–15 minutes. Praise should be moderate and encouraging, not over the top, and should be for specific reading success.
- ❖ *Build experience.* Develop a good book list by visiting your library; provide a reward for books read; introduce family reading or quiet time; allow reading before lights out; tape-record 'before and after' reading practice; ask your child to read a story on to a cassette for a younger sibling; teach breathing at punctuation.

There's a lovely old sign in a bookshop that says it all:
'Richer than I you never can be:
I had a parent who read to me.'

Reading fun and games

Oral practice

Read funny poems, and let your children ham up their reading. Encourage a flowing rhythm and relaxed reading. Pretend to read to an audience. Get your kids to read instead of washing up, and encourage them to read to little kids.

Vocabulary

Play games such as Scrabble, Boggle, Crosswords and Findaword. Give your child a new word book; teach dictionary skills.

Finger pointing

It is okay to finger-point at the words while you read, as this supports the idea of one-to-one matching.

Cloze

Select a passage, then cover every twentieth word or so, which the kids then have to guess. Gradually reduce this to every tenth word. At first you can provide a random list of the missing words; as the children gain confidence, fade out the support list.

Word-attack skills

Teach your child to group sounds together in words from left to right, and not just guess at the word from the first one or two letters.

Comprehension development

❖ Look through the book before asking them to read. Discuss what they think it might be about, and get them to predict what will happen.

❖ Allow the kids time to self-correct, but provide the word after a few moments so that the flow of the story is maintained.

❖ Before turning a page, question the kids as to what they think will happen next – then ask why. Go even further by asking for reasons for this prediction.

❖ After reading, ask the kids to tell the story in their own words and in the right sequence. Use prompts such as 'and then ...'.

❖ Some kids love drawing – have them draw the story sequence in comic or cartoon form.

❖ Have the kids extend the story beyond its ending, or write a new ending, as in the 'Choose your own adventure' books.

❖ Discuss any tricky words in the story before reading it. Knowing what the difficult words mean and how to say them has been shown to lift comprehension by 80 percent!

Sight words

Eighty percent of everything we read contains 'sight' words, or very frequently used words. We have used the Dolch list of sight words to show you the most common ones, grouped vertically in lists of increasing difficulty.

Easy	Hard	Harder
A	All	After
And	Am	Again
Away	Are	An
Big	At	Any
Blue	Ate	As
Can	Be	Ask
Come	Black	By
Down	Brown	Could
Find	But	Every
For	Came	Fly
Funny	Did	From
Go	Do	Give
Help	Eat	Going
Hers	Four	Had
I	Get	Has
In	Good	Her
Is	Has	Him
It	He	How
Jump	Into	Just
Little	Like	Know
Look	Must	Let
Make	New	Live
Me	No	May
My	Now	Of
Not	On	Old

Easy	Hard	Harder
One	Our	Once
Play	Out	Open
Red	Please	Over
Run	Pretty	Put
Said	Ran	Round
See	Ride	Some
The	Saw	Stop
Three	Say	Take
To	She	Thank
Two	So	Them
Up	Soon	Then
We	That	Think
Yellow	There	Walk
You	They	Where
	This	When
	Too	
	Under	
	Want	
	Was	
	Well	
	Went	
	What	
	White	
	Who	
	Will	
	With	
	Yes	

Managing reading difficulties

Remember that all preschoolers and young children have a reading 'problem' – it takes time to get to know this crazy symbol system we call our written language. By about the age of seven or eight, most kids have sufficient neurological maturity and experience with the written word for us to be able to identify genuine problems. In fact, some overseas school systems don't even try to teach kids to read until they're eight!

For any child with reading problems, it is a good idea to have an eye check-up, but get a second opinion if the child has to wear glasses or undertake a program of optometrical exercises. The research is clear: if you want your kids to read better, practise reading!

The reluctant reader

If you have a reluctant reader, first consider what *you* are doing – are you modelling good habits? We can all be reluctant at times, especially when we are being forced into a situation. This really raises the hackles. Many parents unknowingly make children view reading as having to plough through a lengthy novel. But reading is much more than that. Magazines are just as valid – as are recipes, programs from sporting events, short stories, plays and poetry, joke books, emails from relatives read aloud, sporting programs, newspapers – anything that opens the door to more understanding.

A parent says ...

Don't compare siblings: my son, Number One, asked to learn to read in the year before school. My son, Number Two, was just not interested. He thought that was the reason why he was going to 'big school'. Both are now proficient and prolific readers.

Teacher says ...

Don't make the levels a child achieves in a reading program a competition ... or a source of anxiety. Reading does take time – and it is not a race! While levelled reading programs help to grow independent reading skills at the stage suitable for the individual child, they also develop competitive anxiety among mums and dads. No longer is it good for a child to be on the level that is suitable for her; it is more important that she gets off that level as soon as possible! It is easy for parents to fall into the trap of seeing the levels as indicators of their child's brilliance (or lack of it). Parents start to drive kids – and teachers – to move up levels as quickly and as efficiently as the parental ego requires.

A true tale ... the future scientist

Mem Fox, the respected author of *Possum Magic*, tells the story of a mother who, when meeting a leading scientist, mentioned that she wanted her son to become a scientist, too. She asked him what she could do to mentally prepare her son for such a career path. The scientist replied, 'Read him a story'.

The mother laughed politely and then asked, 'But after I've read my son a story, what should I do then?'

The scientist replied, 'Read him another, and another. Nothing stimulates the mind of a child more than reading'.

Get them writing early and often

You would be the exception if you believed that today's kids are better writers than in the pen-and-ink days. Years ago, form, finish, and pride in workmanship were almost as important as educational goals. Now education is expected to deal with a world that's creating and communicating information faster than ever before – and that requires speed and efficiency. The goals have changed and the tools have changed.

The writing focus is now on fluency and legibility, and an easy transition from print to running-writing. Print has shifted from circles and verticals to ellipses and sloped strokes, while running-writing is made by the easiest possible linkage of these foundation forms. How well you write is now about how clearly and fluently you communicate.

If kids enjoy writing and people enjoy what they are communicating, those kids generally become good writers. But if their spelling is poor, or if their fine motor control is poor, they rarely receive praise and tend to lose all enthusiasm for communicating in the written form.

Encourage *two-year-olds* by letting them experiment with a variety of implements on a variety of surfaces (walls excluded, of course). Some good combinations are: chalk on chalkboard, crayon, chubby chalk and textas on paper, detergent foam on plastic, paint on plastic or paper, felt pens on paper, felt pens on whiteboards, fingers in sand, fingers in paint, and charcoal on newspaper.

From the age of two, children will produce some reasonable scribbles and circles, so praise all their efforts just as you would real writing. Even their constipated little scribble blobs, which look like squashed flies, are special to them. One of the first means of communication for your child is through drawing. As kids get older and start to read their own first name or write a cross or a letter as their signature, let them share in sending cards so they are 'in print'. Try to print when putting names on school clothes and equipment, so they see the correct style early.

For *younger writers*, it is all too easy for parents to notice mistakes. Don't draw attention to the errors – focus more on the content and the ideas that are being expressed. Being praised for the effort, a young writer will want to go further and write more.

Encourage *older kids* to do lots of writing of cards, shopping lists and letters. Let them use a wide variety of implements so that their writing keeps its freshness. Give them a container for their desk that can hold different types of pens and pencils so they can decorate their work and enjoy the end results.

How to encourage good writing habits

- Don't force a young writer to stay in between the lines on a page.
- Encourage writing in every form that grabs your child's interest – ask her to help write the shopping list while you call out the items, send postcards to family and friends when on holidays, keep a diary of special events, write plays, make name-tags and signs for things at home.
- Encourage your child to use a word processor or to play games on-screen using the mouse to form figures or letters.
- Display drawings and writing that your child has done at school.
- If their writing is too heavy or smeary, a different pencil grade or pen point could help.
- If you have a 'leftie' (which is about a one-in-ten chance), remember that writing from left to right is harder. With modern ballpoints, these children can use the same grip as the right-handers – that is, pinching between thumb and index finger and resting it on the middle one. But left-handers should have a multidirectional-grip pen, and should hold it a bit further back so they can see what they are writing. The page should be left of centre, too, for easier access and better posture.
- If your kids are developing backache or neckache, their chair is either too low or too soft, or they are leaning too far over the page. Technically, the head should not be tilted too far forward, elbows should be level with the table, the seat should be firm, the feet comfortably on the floor, and the non-writing arm should take the weight to allow the writing arm to glide over the writing surface.

▶ If your child is writing with her head too close, or at an angle to the page, or with eyes partially shut, make an appointment with an optometrist or ophthalmologist.

▶ If you have tried everything for years and your child still doesn't write well, then maybe – as soon as finances allow – you should cut your losses and invest in a computer. These days there is a strong emphasis on children using computers to publish their writing at school, with the consequence that there is less need for 'neat' handwriting. It also helps in the presentation of assignments and essays, and prevents the loss of marks because of untidiness or illegibility.

Teacher says ...

A good idea for children struggling with the written language is to get them to 'story-board'. With a digital camera, your child can photograph a story and then place the pictures in order using the computer. This helps promote sequencing, and leads to a better understanding of paragraphs and details. Then get the child to write captions about what is happening. You can supply interesting words and develop the child's sentences.

Write it right

Remember those old writing lessons: 'Watch me, now write it in the air, now write it on your page, now do a line of them … '. They were terrific when there was plenty of time, but this approach didn't help when the pace was on, and it wasn't much use in high school. Effort comes from enjoyment, and pride comes from success, so if a child's spelling is off, or her written ideas aren't appreciated, then her writing is very likely to be wretched.

As mentioned, position and posture are vital in the early stages of learning to write. If your child's head is too low when writing, then, as stated, it may be a vision problem, so see an optometrist. And if your child's head is level with the page and her eyes are shut, then it's time to see a psychologist!

Keeping them writing

In addition, consider getting a portfolio of writing. Keep a selection of writing over the course of time. You might choose two pieces per year. Slowly build up a collection of writing. Photocopy this 'best work' and your comments about why it was chosen, and put it all in a good-quality journal. This portfolio will highlight your child's improvements, increase motivation and give you a great discussion focus. It also makes a great twenty-first-birthday or wedding present. As the writing improves, let the child tell you why. You might offer some special privilege as an incentive (even a calligraphy set if she is becoming keen and proud).

Another good idea is to use Photostory, a free software program from Microsoft that allows children to make slideshows. They can add music and their own captions.

The reluctant writer

Writing involves a combination of many physical and mental processes. It can be tough work, especially when you are not overly thrilled about having to fill a blank page. But extra practice is what the reluctant writer needs. Remember that there are many different types of texts children can imitate. For some reluctant writers, try using limericks or short poetry, jokes, captions to pictures they draw, or get them to start a journal. Or you could get them to write the lyrics to their favourite songs – copying from what they hear. Then get them to write their own song or poem.

A parent says ...

I have a son who is a reluctant writer. He needs lots of reassurance about the value of his ideas. He is a bit of a perfectionist, always wanting to hone every single line he writes to make it 'perfect'. We continually encourage him by focusing on the overall idea – getting him to discuss what will happen next and leading him away from just focusing on a line at a time. We also have to reassure him that mistakes are learning opportunities. We tell him that making mistakes are positive learning tools and part of the writing process.

Prompting

You can prompt in reading, and the same is true of writing. Be excited and positive about each attempt at writing, and help your child to reflect on what she has written by prompting with questions like:

* ❖ 'Say the sentence to yourself. Does it sound right? Does it look right?'
* ❖ 'Choose a word and say it slowly and clearly. What do you hear? How do you write it?' (Repeat this, focusing on other sounds.)
* ❖ 'Do you know another word for _____?'

Improving your child's writing

▶ Use graphic organisers – templates that allow a child to plan a piece of work (see http://www.readwritethink.org/student_mat/index.asp).

▶ Cut out cartoons and paste them into a magazine, then have your child create the text and speech bubbles.

▶ Use mind-map ideas – if you don't know what a mind map is, Google it.

▶ Use the writing process – plan, draft, edit. But be aware that many children want to write simply to communicate – they don't like having to go back and edit. You can overcome this by choosing a writing task that 'has' to be neat – such as a thank-you letter or email. This places the importance on the person the child is writing to, such as a grandparent.

▶ Use mnemonics to remind children about the writing process, e.g. 'POWER' ('plan, organise, write the draft, edit, revise').

▶ If you are keen to improve your child's writing structure, then find her best piece of writing and discuss it in terms of:
   – neatness
   – even letter heights
   – well-made letters
   – placement on the line, not above or through it, and
   – the amount of crossing-out.

▶ For the younger writer, praise every effort and focus on what is right rather than what is wrong. This encourages positive improvement.

▶ Young children are very keen on writing letters to friends – don't force this, just supply good stationery.

▶ Provide a variety of ideas for them to write about – from themselves to fantasy to real-life stories. Keep a list of stories. Tell made-up stories to your children while they are eating breakfast in the morning.

▶ Talk at home about a topic that your child may be able to write about at school. Encouraging a little practice at home helps to ensure more success at school.

▶ If getting kids to express thoughts and ideas in writing is the goal, rather than who is the neatest writer, use the computer – most kids love it.

Teacher says ...

A great way to improve writing is to focus on shortening the plot. When a child first wants to write, he or she will have a lengthy outline of ideas joined together with 'and then ...' followed by many more 'and then's. Many early efforts start with waking up in the morning 'and then' going down to breakfast 'and then' eating breakfast; ask your child to think of the most exciting part and to focus on that. You can get even better results from older children by asking them to imagine they are filming a movie – you have paid them $1,000,000 for just the opening scene. You want them to 'show' you the movie on the big screen. Get them to talk it through and then get them to write it down. Discussion is a great prompt for good writing!

Understanding spelling

English has adopted many words from different languages and cultures over time. As a result, it doesn't make sense: just when you think you know how to spell one word using a 'rule', up pops another with a different 'rule'. Consider the following:

❖ 'Since there is no time like the present, she thought it was time to present the present.'
❖ 'I did not object to the object.'
❖ 'They were too close to the door to close it.'
❖ 'The wind was too strong to wind in the sail.'
❖ 'The dove dove down out of the sky.'
❖ 'The bandage was wound around the wound.'

Spelling and reading are closely related, but not identical; reading calls for only the recognition of words (such as 'once'), but spelling poses the harder task of correct recall. If a child cannot recall a word to spell it, it's not just laziness – some can't work out the sounds, while others can't work out the teacher. Every such child deserves help.

Spelling strategies

The most important thing here is to add variety – routines have a habit of losing the essence of learning something. Be creative. Here are a few strategies to help:

'Look Say Cover Write Check' – this is the most commonly used strategy. The child has a list of words and then has to copy the words after going through this process. Warning: using this system to learn long lists can become very tedious for children, who end up thinking more about finishing the list than learning the words.

Letter Pyramids – this is for difficult words. Write down the whole word. Directly under it, write down the word minus the first letter. Directly under that, write down the word minus the first two letters.

Continue until you have no more letters. You can use this method leaving out letters from the beginning or the end, e.g.:

W	O	R	D	or	W	O	R	D
	O	R	D		W	O	R	
		R	D		W	O		
			D		W			

Highlight the hard parts – this is for learning words that have a difficult string of letters. Colour those parts or write them bigger to stand out, e.g.:

sep**ar**ate

Word traces – draw outlines around the letters to show the shape of the word, e.g.:

Plasticine word models – model words in plasticine or play dough. You can use different colours to highlight special letter patterns.

Over-pronounce words – research has highlighted the importance of stressing letter sounds in words. For example, when saying out loud the word 'beautiful', say it as

B E A **YOU** Ti FUL

How you can help with spelling

❖ The best way to help is to provide plenty of good, fun books from the early picture-book stage, so the letters and patterns keep hammering away at the memory. By the age of three, many children can recognise their own name; by five, if children have taught themselves to write their first name, they will probably be problem-free spellers.

❖ If the patterns are just not sticking, and tempers at homework time are becoming heated, it may be helpful to share that frustration with the teacher and ask for some better strategies. Raising your voice or your blood pressure is guaranteed to also raise poorer spellers.

❖ If you want to give your children some fun spelling games, ask at your local educational book supplier. One long-time favourite book is *Teach Your Child to Spell*. It shows how big words are carved up into small, easy-to-remember units, for example, 'cat-er-pill-ar'. By using two or three words from the school spelling list in a 15-minute session per day, kids will learn to carve up words and recall one part at a time. This approach involves sight, sound and touch, and makes your child feel successful.

Teacher says ...

Always ask a child who can't spell a word to imagine she can see it – written on a fridge or as a special sign in bright colours. Get your child to concentrate on seeing the word before spelling the word – give her cues and links to similar word families, but don't 'tell' her how to spell the word. Then, when she does get it, make special mention that you didn't actually tell her, that *she* was able to spell the word – she just needed the right strategy. She needed to 'think smarter'.

Spelling problem checklist

Look at a story your 'problem speller' has written and try to pick up the pattern of errors. Remember that all young kids have a spelling 'problem' as they try to cope with the variations of our language and its many complex rules, so don't be making young kids anxious when they don't need to be. However, primary-school kids *could* be considered to have a spelling problem if they have one or more of the following difficulties:

- learns words but can't remember them days or weeks later
- can only remember a list if the words are kept in the same order
- spells words differently at different times
- spells words as they sound but can't remember what they look like
- can't see errors in spelling
- can't break a word into parts or syllables
- can recall sounds but can't recall symbols or combinations
- uses incorrect pronunciation in spelling (e.g. 'fin' for 'thin'), and
- confuses the order of letters in spelling (e.g. 'gril' for 'girl').

Managing spelling problems

We can't all spell well, but we can all learn strategies that help us improve. Being a 'good' speller means having a well-equipped toolbox, with smart solutions at hand.

Error	Possible solution
Reasonable phonic errors, e.g. 'dorter' for 'daughter'.	Use word error flashcards (i.e. with correct and incorrect spellings) and lots of reading to cement correct letter patterns.
Unreasonable phonic errors, e.g. 'mothu' for 'mother'.	Help to learn word families; teach the child to listen carefully; play 'sound detective' games (e.g. 'Which word sounds different – thin, thin, fin, thin?').
Letter transpositions, e.g. 'gril' 'for girl'.	Play word drill games, work on root blends (e.g. '-ir'); use gimmicky memory aids (e.g. 'I are a girl.').
Auditory errors, e.g. 'fin' for 'thin'.	Tape-record the child reading and let her pick the errors; practise correct speech into a tape recorder.
Handwriting reversals, e.g. 'bug' for 'dug'.	Use gimmicky memory aids to help the child remember the difference (e.g. 'bat before ball'). Or say that 'b' has a line before the ball – and our lips join together to make a line when we say 'b'.
Repetition, e.g. 'positition'.	Provide self-correction incentives such as five minutes' extra TV time for each spelling error they spot for themselves; practise re-reading words.
Unclassifiable, e.g. 'dta' for 'daughter'.	Give easier work and praise for success; practise listening to word sequences.

DO ...

❖ encourage all attempts at spelling: 'Have a go ...'
❖ make spelling fun – play games
❖ use an alphabet strip with pictures to assist young spellers to find the sound they need

- focus on achievable words first – success breeds success
- show the kids how to use dictionaries, encyclopedias and thesauruses – there are now many online sites that are excellent for this (e.g. http://dictionary.com), and
- surround your child's world with print (e.g. share story books, kitchen reminders, bedroom wall-hangings, of verse, etc.) – the more the child sees the word, the more likely it is to imprint on the mind.

DON'T tell your child the correct spelling – tempting as that may be, it will encourage spelling dependency habits that could last a lifetime, and will put similar demands on the teacher. Some parents and teachers use a three-step process (set out as three columns on a page) – the child's first attempt, the second attempt after consulting a dictionary or other spelling sources, and then the teacher's input, if needed.

A true tale ... Mark

Carolyn threw Mark's spelling book down.

'I've had enough! We learn them and go over them ... now look at what he wrote in his story, which has really upset his father.'

Reece often got his b's and d's mixed up, and instead of writing 'Dad likes to drink beer', he wrote 'Dad likes to brink deer' – and, as Mum said, Dad's not even a member of the Shooters Party!

Some poor spellers are word-blind: they can't remember what a word looks like, and have to sound it out every time. Other kids are sound-deaf: they can write out words they've seen, but they can't sound them out for love or money.

But young Mark had become quite clever at covering his problem. When he went away to camp, he wrote to his mum that his tent was covered in 'little snakes'. She rang in hysterics, only to discover that he just couldn't spell 'caterpillars'.

Breaking down the Maths barrier

Just the dull, flat sound of the word 'Maths' can depress anyone who doesn't get a thrill from mental gymnastics with figures and numbers. However, such negativity is a learned attitude. Most young kids enjoy learning to count; they find the rhythm and precision very satisfying. There are many ways parents can help kids without pumping out rote numbers. Every time you ask your child to put something back where it belongs, or sort out cutlery, or silver and gold coins, she is learning to put things in groups – and that's Maths. Organising her packing for holidays, managing time to play and work, getting ready for school on time, saving pocket money to buy things, predicting what will happen if/when ... that's Maths, too, and it should be fun.

Sometimes kids do well in the early grades and then drop back, not because the work is boring but because they might have a reading problem: the older kids get, the more word-based Maths is.

Maths problem checklist

If your child struggles at Maths, don't promote self-doubt by saying within earshot that she 'can't do Maths'. And don't panic if your child cannot count back from ten by twos. Instead, review the following guidelines for five- and seven-year-olds as indicators.

Your child may have a problem with mathematical thinking if, by the age of *five*, she:

▶ can't rote-count to ten
▶ can't count simple objects, like blocks up to five
▶ can't keep to the correct counting order
▶ can't tell which names go with which numbers up to ten
▶ mixes up colours
▶ mixes up shapes, or
▶ thinks coins are all just pieces of money, with no difference in value.

Your child may have a problem with mathematical thinking if, by the age of *seven*, she:

▶ writes numbers back to front
▶ hates doing Maths homework
▶ can't understand the difference between big and little, under and over, or first and last
▶ is behind friends and classmates
▶ can only calculate with her fingers
▶ still doesn't know the days of the week
▶ has no real idea of time, or
▶ has difficulty following a set of instructions.

A true tale ... Andy

Andy was always good at Drama and English, but hopeless at Maths. When he was brought in for assessment and tutoring, his father, Dave, mentioned that he had had a similar problem, which was why he'd gone into Law. We joked (with a touch of envy on my part) that surely lawyers needed to know how much they were banking. Dave got help for Andy before the problem became a huge mathematical chip on Andy's shoulder. When we last reviewed Andy's progress, he was in the middle-ability Maths class at high school.

Teacher says ...

▮ Play numbers-based games with the kids – Ludo, Bingo, etc.
▮ Encourage help with prices and quantities when shopping.
▮ Never say, 'I wasn't any good, either' or 'I hated Maths, too'. This tells the child that it's okay to dislike it or to fail.
▮ A book useful for upper-primary and secondary students is *A Mathematical Dictionary for Schools* (see Authors' notes). It contains definitions and examples of the mathematical words likely to be encountered.

How you can help with Maths

❖ Maths is one special area that can be easily and tangibly helped by computer assistance. In fact, some would say that for this particular topic, computers can do a better job than humans – they go at the right pace, they're very forgiving, they don't get frustrated, and they work at individual levels for every child. There are now some fabulous games on computer that can make Maths fun – even for three-year-olds who can 'work the mouse'. But if a child is starting to give you the 'I can't do it' treatment, then see the teacher and find out in which areas she is having trouble. Our strong suggestion is to arrange some tutoring: it helps to lift children's marks and their morales in a hurry before they can dismiss Maths, as many parents (particularly mums) tend to do. Of all the remedial subjects, Maths is the one that responds most readily and noticeably to stimulating, caring, praising, yet emotionally uninvolved tutors. It's also the most responsive to regular practice, and that's where computer games can do the job so well.

❖ An Australian-made program that is taking the world by storm is Mathletics (http://mathletics.com). It has different levels of difficulty, and children from around the world challenge each other in groups of four to complete set questions in a timed period. Boys love this program, which requires only an Internet connection and an annual subscription.

❖ Some teachers swear by series such as 'Maths Made Easy' (available on CD-Rom), which offer children the chance to select from the menu of activities they want further work in (e.g. fractions), with different disks for every grade of primary school.

❖ As there are so many series around, you'd be wise to link up with what's being used in your children's school. 'Rainforest Maths' (http://www.rainforestmaths.com) is a good, free, Australian-made product, or try some of the free games online at http://www.counton.org/games, and any of the 'Maths Blaster' series for drill and practice.

- There are also many free sites that use manipulatives – i.e. programs that allow a child to see Maths in action ... by doing! A great site is http://nlvm.usu.edu/en/nav/vlibrary.html, where you can select the area of need.
- Another great free site for learning tables and getting printed feedback is http://www.gdbdp.com/multiflyer/play_online.html. It blasts the children through the Solar System while they answer their tables, then gives a print-out of their strengths and weaknesses.

You still need to make it personal

All these sites are amazing, but it must be pointed out that most children respond best to personal, professional, one-to-one help with an individualised program designed by their teacher and tutor – preferably together.

Strategies for thinking mathematically

Here is a list of the main mathematical strategies our kids are using today.

Rainbow number
patterns: These use
coloured cards to represent
whole numbers up to ten.
Have the same colours
for number patterns
that add up to make ten.
Then draw rainbow lines
to show how these link.
This will help develop a
basic understanding of
'ten' facts.

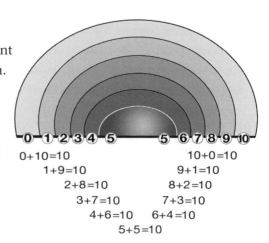

0+10=10   10+0=10
1+9=10   9+1=10
2+8=10   8+2=10
3+7=10   7+3=10
4+6=10   6+4=10
5+5=10

Jump strategy: An addition or subtraction strategy in which the
student places the first number on an *empty number line* and then
counts forward or backwards, firstly by tens and then by ones
to perform a calculation. The number of jumps will reduce with
increased understanding.

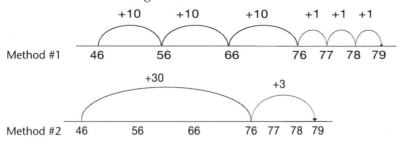

Split strategy: This is breaking down two-digit numbers so you deal
with the tens and the ones separately, e.g.

$$74 + 25 = (70 + 20) + (4 + 5) = 90 + 9 = 99$$

Doubles strategy: This has children adding or subtracting doubles, e.g.

$$7 + 6 = (6 + 6) + 1 = 12 + 1 = 13$$
$$9 - 5 - 4 + (5 - 5) - 4$$

Compensation method: This has children building up to groups of tens –referred to as 'rounding up'. We compensate by building up or down to form a whole ten group. For instance:

Addition: $109 + 23 = (110 + 23) - 1$ or $93 + 38 = (90 + 38) + 3$

The compensation method is not just for additions.

Subtraction: $84 - 9 = (84 - 10) + 1$

Notice how again we are making a group of ten.

Multiplication: $9 \times 6 = (10 \times 6) - (1 \times 6)$.

Compensating to create a multiple of ten makes the sum easier to figure out.

Subtraction thinking: Subtraction questions such as $3000 - 2593$ can be handled mentally by subtracting 1 from 3000 and 1 from 2593. By taking this approach, the subtraction no longer requires any 'borrowing', e.g.

$3000 - 2593 = (3000 - 1) - (2593 - 1) = 2999 - 2592 = 407$

'Storekeeper' thinking (adding to subtract): Subtraction can be done by adding. Say you want to do $143 - 84$. Start by thinking of the reverse: $84 + ? = 143$. Next, think what goes with 84 to make 100 and then add on the rest to this total, e.g.

Add 16 to 84 to reach 100.

Add 43 to 100 to reach 143.

The answer to the subtraction is $16 + 43 = 59$.

The decomposition method: Many parents will be confronted by this different method of subtracting. Whereas many of us 'oldies' learnt to use the trading method, the decomposition method focuses on the child's awareness of groups of tens and place value.

Step 1:
$4 - 7$ can't do. Borrow a ten from the three tens. This leaves 2 tens and 14 digits.

Step 2:
2 tens – 6 tens can't do. Borrow a ten from the 1 hundred. This makes 12 tens and 9 hundreds.

Part Four

Thriving in the playground

'An understanding heart is everything as a teacher, and cannot be esteemed highly enough. One looks back with appreciation to the brilliant teachers, but with gratitude to those who touched our human feeling. The curriculum is so much necessary raw material, but warmth is the vital element for the growing plant and for the soul of the child.'

Carl Jung

As far as young kids are concerned, the playground is where it all happens – it's the nerve centre of the school. Tempting as it is to shield children from playground problems, we must remember that we are all basically social creatures. Our happiness largely depends on how well we can negotiate our style, values, attitudes and beliefs within the social network, rather than opting for isolation.

This Part explores the world of free play for kids. We will share our thoughts on how to get kids involved and how to support them if they feel isolated, and we will lift the lid on the key issues surrounding bullying and cyber-bullying.

Loneliness

Parent: *'My son keeps coming home from school saying he has no-one to play with. I feel so sorry for him, but what can I do?'*

Suggestions:

1. Don't take over. We've all had to weather some tough times, and we are the better for it. Just express your confidence in his ability to beat *his* problem. Don't promote dependence.

2. Really listen to what he's saying and then reflect what you think he's *feeling* (sad, angry, etc.) rather than focusing on the content. This keeps you in touch and conveys to him that you care.

3. Help him problem-solve a few ways out of his loneliness, for example, what he could do to get kids to play with him.

4. Set a time limit of, say, a week to check how well the plan is working.

5. If the plan is proceeding well, refine it; if it isn't, set up some new tactics or perhaps talk to someone like your son's teacher or counsellor, not only for ideas but also to find out what's going wrong.

Teacher says ...

Be prepared for kids to try various activities until they find what suits their style, because many shy children just don't believe they are good at anything. Encourage their independence, and don't allow them to use you as their 'shyness cover' too often.

What kids say about loneliness

'You get lonely when you don't have friends or there's no-one to talk to or you're left out.'

'I think kids don't want to play with me because of the way I look.'

'When my mum or dad think I've been bad, they send me to my room for a long time, and that is a very lonely place to be when you're sad.'

'When my cat died was the loneliest time for me ever.'

'I never feel lonely because I've always got myself.'

'When my two friends go off and leave me with no-one ...'

'If I'm left out at a party it is bad enough, if I'm not invited I feel even worse.'

'When my parents fight and talk about divorce, I just want to cry and feel like I wish that I had never been born.'

Isolated play

Parent: *'My son sometimes plays well with other kids, but often he says he just wants to play cars or do something on his own. Should I be worried?'*

Some kids are simply self-sufficient and don't appear to need friends as much as others do. As long as they know how to mix, how to share, how to work with others, and how to enjoy fun with others, they don't have a problem, particularly if all the other indicators show they are pretty happy and well adjusted.

'Bad' friends

Parent: *'I know I shouldn't pick my child's friends, but I really get worried about some of the dreadful kids she is mixing with. I've heard some terrible stories. What should I do?'*

Suggestions:

❖ Like it or not, you can't pick your children's friends, and if you try to 'unpick' a friendship, it frequently makes a child more determined to keep it.

❖ Try not to make your daughter choose between friends and family. Sometimes success is achieved by role reversal – when 'friends' have done something nasty to her, ask her would a friend do that, would she do that, to someone she liked. This can alert her to the fact that she is putting more into the friendship than her 'friend' is.

❖ If she says her friends are good, use logical consequences – if they're 'good' friends, they'll make you feel good and act 'good'. If that's not happening, it throws the problem into stark relief.

❖ Invite the 'bad' friends over to get to know them. They may be better than you think, and they may get better if they like the contact with you.

❖ Have confidence that your basic training will win out in the long run, and remember that all kids have to learn through trial and (hopefully only a little) error.

Friend-finding fundamentals

Find your child's strengths.

Reassure your child that everyone is looking for friends.

Instil your confidence in his ability to find a friend.

Encourage positive attempts to make friends.

Never take over, publicise your child's problem, or 'buy' friends.

Discourage analysis and encourage action to meet other kids.

Share your own similar experiences and positive outcomes.

Have a talk to the teacher about class activities to enhance friendships.

Invite friends with similar-aged kids for a day out.

Praise any success.

Stop any home hindrances (e.g. overprotection, overindulgence).

Teacher says ...

One thing that really hurts friendships is when there is a party and the invitations are handed out in class to all the children except for one or two. This is a hard one, because the parents and the birthday child 'own' the party. The best advice is to invite everyone if you are having a 'class party'. Leaving just one or two children out is really upsetting, and those kids do remember.

Bullying – the basics

Nothing undermines our task of helping kids thrive at school more than the disastrous and soul-destroying impact of bullying. Of course kids have to learn how to cope with the good, the bad and the ugly – that's life. But feeling bullied makes learning unattainable, disagreeable and downright painful. For parents, a child coming home clearly upset and distraught from an incident at school is confronting. A sound piece of advice is to *work with the school* – don't rush into phone calls with other kids' parents. As with any emotional experience, take a deep breath and count to three – hundred! Then read this section on bullying.

A true tale ... name-calling

Teaching in Sydney is a wonderful experience. It is such a diverse place. After lunch one day, Anton rushed into our English lesson sobbing and furious. He blurted out that Niko had called him gay. This was just too much to bear – Anton was inconsolable. The first thing to do was to find out the facts. With hands open wide, pleading for all to hear, Niko swore he hadn't called Anton gay.

Anton then howled at him, 'You did! You *did* call me gay!' Between breaths and sobs, he added, 'Ask the others.'

This was a recipe for a disaster: tit-for-tatting would consume the entire English lesson. Instead, I got the boys to write down their accounts in isolation. At least they were learning how to write reports! A pencil and paper were provided. It wasn't long before there was a timid knock at the door and Niko's sanguine face stared in.

'Sir, can I see you?'

'Yes, Niko – what is it that you have to say?'

'Sir, please, my father will be very angry. He can be a very angry man. I do not want any trouble.'

'Niko, you have made your own trouble – Anton is very upset. He says you called him gay. This is not acceptable.'

'Sir, I swear – I did not say he was gay. All I said was that he was a homeless sexual!'

What to do after a bullying incident

1 The first thing to do is to determine whether the incident is in fact 'bullying'. Unfortunately, what we once considered 'teasing' is now called bullying. Bullying is an ongoing, intimidating and purposeful act intended to humiliate.

2 There are always two sides. Listen to all the information, but understand that your child will come home with revelations of incidents that, to his perception, are totally true (the other kids involved will be doing exactly the same with their parents). These incidents may be bullying, or your child may have been involved in a dispute over a decision in handball at lunchtime.

3 If it is a one-off case and your child is upset, comfort him until calm. Then 'rewind' the situation together and look for 'escape routes'. It is important that parents don't take over the problem from the child – it is *his* problem, so he has to solve it. But keep monitoring things.

4 If it is bullying – *ACT*. If it is ongoing, you may not be confronted by a sad and distraught child until way into the bullying cycle. Many kids don't want to 'trouble' their parents – although mums are usually the first to find out. Comfort your child and tell him that you won't allow this to happen – be solid. Then discuss the bully's behaviour – turn it on the other child(ren): after all, they are the ones with social problems.

5 Talk to the teacher with your child in a three-way discussion to come up with a solution that has the greatest support and awareness of all parties. Then organise a review. Research shows that the best way to deal with bullying is to get bystanders to stand up and do what is right. This is best done by a class coming up with its own code of conduct. This way, the children assert their own rules for their behaviour – that is, they learn to take ownership and responsibility.

Bullying facts and fantasies

Research conducted in 2007 by the University of Western Sydney found that one in six high-schoolers is bullied every week, and one in ten is a bully. Being a bully increases by six times the chance of having a criminal conviction by the age of eighteen.

Bullying can take many forms:

- ❖ physical – blows, kicks, pushing
- ❖ gestural – intimidating or threatening actions and gestures
- ❖ verbal – name-calling and abusive comments
- ❖ indirect – deliberately not including someone or removing their belongings, and
- ❖ relational – setting up others to hurt or ostracise someone.

Most people think that bullies have low self-esteem. In fact, often the bully feels good about bullying, especially if it makes him popular (or feared) at school. Bullies often possess one of two distinct types of personality: dominant (the alpha male or female), or seeking dominance via humiliation (as they have low self-esteem). And research from Norway suggests that parents of bullies show some common traits: a lack of time for, and interest in, the child's early years; too much tolerance of aggressive behaviour; and frequent use of physical punishment for 'discipline'.

Intervention needs to happen at the first signs of behaviour that seeks to deliberately and repeatedly humiliate or hurt other children. The research from Norway reports real success when parents and teachers work together with common attitudes and a zero-tolerance outlook. This includes an absolute insistence on decent behaviour, backed up by non-physical punishments such as the denial of television, sport, transport, pocket money or whatever pleasures parents have control over.

A true tale ... Luke

Luke was a fighter. At the age of seven, he could flatten any kid in Infants school. But the more he hit, the more he was hated, and the more heated he became. His language was foul, his friends were few, and the school was fed up – they were ready to kick him out.

Everyone's recipe to cure him failed – the school tried detention; the family tried deprivation; but *no-one* tried inspiration. Luke's world was just as negative about him as he was about it.

So Mum began to create a different world around him. She used television time to gain cooperation in family chores, with the further incentive of giving him a choice of jobs. His dad tied a fishing trip to a good weekly report from school; the teacher linked spending lunchtime with the other kids to a 'hit-free' day – otherwise he would be sent to the office. And we arranged for him to learn Zen Bu Kan to smarten up his self-control.

A while back Luke brought in his reports and a scrapbook bursting with merit certificates for good behaviour. His mum reckons that the first hint of success made him hungry for more, and then the whole positive approach just snowballed.

Stop being a target

Some kids live in enormous fear of bullies – it can be so bad that their sleep, appetite and health suffers, and they become depressed. If your child is always the target, chances are that he needs to learn how to avoid contact with bullies, how to assert the message for the bully to 'back off' if confronted, how to stop aggravating bullies (however innocently), and, as a back-up, maybe some self-defence tactics (but be warned: advertised skills attract challengers). Whatever the tactics, the message must be that bullying is not acceptable.

Targets can help themselves

Good strategies for targets include the following:

▶ examining their own behaviour to make sure that they ooze confidence and don't cower like a victim or stir other kids

▶ controlling their own fear so they're not easily intimidated – this can be done, for instance, by counting the number of times the bully tries to upset them in word or deed, with the goal being that, by counting rather than reacting, the daily score will fall because the taunt is being wasted

▶ telling someone in authority and not being put off by a bully's threats to 'get' them if they dob, or tell – bullying is a form of assault

▶ calling the bully's bluff by telling him why they think he is bothering them

▶ exposing the jugular – acknowledging that the bully could beat them in a fight and, in so doing, take the combat incentive away

▶ depriving the bully of opportunity – for instance, if the bully is taking their lunch money, bring lunch from home (not money)

▶ reducing points of contact – playing in places and going places where they know the bully does not hang out

▶ networking – finding someone older and respected by the bully to act as friend and protector, but not as bodyguard

▶ making friends – some bullies are unhappy, so offering friendship can sometimes be a way to settle the problem

▶ developing assertiveness skills (see below), and

▶ drawing on the bystanders, who are the key to resolving bullying issues in a school.

You can help by building friendships with your child's classmates and their parents.

Being assertive

Targets need to learn assertiveness skills – and, believe it or not, so do bullies! Many bullies are using aggression to get their way when the proper use of assertiveness could achieve the same end without doing damage to other people. Being assertive means:

❖ considering the other person's feelings and reactions

❖ staying calm and standing your ground

❖ keeping your rights and respecting the rights of others, and

❖ taking responsibility for your own actions.

Notice that the 3Rs we mentioned in Part Two – respect, responsibility, and relationships and social connections – once again come to the fore!

Tease-tossing tactics

Select the style that best suits your child's personality and the circumstances.

Fogging

This technique involves kids using words designed to direct the bully's attention away from what is happening, e.g. if a bully keeps taking another child's pencil case from the desk, the target might say, 'I'm so glad you like my pencil case. Do you want to know where I bought it?'

Deflation

This involves raising the target's self-esteem and self-image enough to make him realise it's the bully who has the problem (this may require professional help). The target can then be armed with a repertoire of standard phrases to deflate a verbal attack. That could be by just agreeing with the bully, or by using phrases such as 'Whatever you reckon' or 'You're probably right' and then moving away from the scene. This works very well with handling rumours!

Dr John's 'tease-tossing tactic' – the 'triple T program'

A favourite technique is to get targets to say all the hurtful names they're being called ('fatso', 'idiot', 'lame brain', 'dickhead', etc.). The secret is to practise pushing them, giggling at them and calling them those names, and they have to count (aloud) how many times we've tried to hurt by word or action. When they have the score correct, then practise counting them silently. When that is working well, set them loose to sidle up alongside a bully and test the technique. After they get home, they put the total for the day on the calendar. Providing the target is mentally set and eager to play the game, their bullying score should be near zero within three weeks. If they feel no-one likes them, use the variation of counting how many kids are nice to them and how many nice things they say to others – and startle them with the change over the three-week period.

Escalated assertiveness

If the bullying is particularly vicious and focused, this technique may be used. It involves raising the voice and explaining the worst consequences of the bully's action if it goes on. For example, if a bully keeps pestering another student by repeatedly hitting or throwing things at him, the target can at first simply say, 'Get lost'. If it's still happening, the next level of response might be, 'Your choice, either get lost or get into trouble', and then move away. If it continues, then the target carries out his proposed course of action of informing the teacher.

Demanding responsibility

This technique is used in conjunction with some of the others, and involves the target asking the bully to correct their behaviour. For example: 'You're harassing me and it's not right. I demand that you stop and apologise'. In the everyday terms the kids are more likely to use, this converts to something like: 'You're bugging me and it's giving me the shits. Get lost and get a life.'

A true tale ... Sam

The older kids at school had been calling ten-year-old Sam names, and would take away his tennis ball unless he told them how great they were, did up their shoelaces, or kissed their feet. If you think that's weird, you should realise that it's happening in some form or another in every school in the country. Good teasers are like predators: they often hunt in packs and pick out a lonely target for attack. Some kids tease to create a stir, some because they are bored, others because they hate anyone who's different, and still others do it for a gang giggle. But the most serious cases are because someone's hurting *them*, so they choose someone who can't fight back as their target.

In Sam's case, we used a multi-pronged strategy for beating the teasing:

❖ We supplied him with a few cartons of second-hand tennis balls. Sam now had the confidence to know that if he lost one, there were more at home, so he had no need to panic.

❖ We taught him to use the 'Tease-tossing tactics' described above.

❖ We decided that if the teasing became too hot to handle, he would casually move the game closer to the playground teacher, so that the 'stirrers' would be less comfortable about overt victimisation.

Sam carried out his plan, and within three days all the harassment had stopped.

Teacher says ...

I'm a school principal, and I've just been hearing on talkback radio a mother blaming the schools for not protecting her child from bullies. She said that her child had now been to six schools, public and private, and they were all the same. Sometimes parents have a different social agenda to schools – they expect different things – so unless the parents and principal sit down and get common ground, not only will each be disappointed by the other, but the child becomes the big loser and may never recover.

If bullying is happening at school, or to and from school, the teacher wants to know about it. Teachers can be very subtle about helping out the situation without letting the bully know who dobbed.

A true tale ... beating school bullying

If you're worried about schoolyard bullies, then you'll be interested to learn that schools are starting to stop the rot. One school we've heard about canvassed its students as to what rights they would like to have at school. The kids' top requests were: not to be made fun of, to expect people to be kind, not to be made sad, not to be scared of teachers, to have friends, not to be scared to come to school, and to be safe.

This all seems reasonable, but now the kids want to take it further, to make sure it actually happens. Any reported violations are brought to the attention of the elected student 'magistrate', who might issue an 'out of court' caution. Repeat offenders are brought before the kids' court, asked why they are doing it and how they intend to make restitution. The court then recommends to the teachers the penalties the kids have agreed on.

Getting *all* of the students involved in this way means that the majority of kids, who had previously been bystanders to bullying incidents, can no longer simply stand by and see their own rules being flaunted. The kids are keen, the teachers are keen. It will be interesting to see how some parents react to their precious bullying darlings being hauled in front of the kids' court. In fact, this entire process should be quite revealing, because most of the bullies I've met over the years have felt like targets themselves, and are also hurting.

The problem with parents is that they blame their kids' problems on everything except heredity.

Cyber-bullying

Sadly, the passing of notes in class has just got a lot nastier. Technology now offers many insidious ways of bullying and discriminating against others without the need to face the person. From the safety of home, children are sending texts and posting information that is truly offensive. And in the security of *their* home, unprepared, other children are reading soul-destroying taunts that have global circulation. This is the frightening reality that many of our children are experiencing ... and doing! The scary part for our kids is that they claim they can't tell their parents – if they do, parents are likely to ban the computer, and for today's younger generation, the computer (data, chat rooms, games, etc.) is their social lifeblood.

What is cyber-bullying?

Cyber-bullying is any communication activity using cyber technology that could be considered harmful. It includes communication via mobile phones (including the spoken word, text messaging, chat, picture and video messaging) and Internet-based communication (including chat rooms, discussion boards, newsgroups, emails and websites). The cyber-bullying can come in many forms and can involve harassment, exclusion, outing, masquerading, aliases, cyber-stalking, etc.

Some sobering Internet statistics

If you think your kids wouldn't be into that sort of thing, maybe you're right. But the research paints a different picture: an 'Online Safety for Teens' survey reveals the following:

❖ Forty-three percent of teenage boys have downloaded files that they didn't want their parents to know about.
❖ Fifty percent of parents believe they always know what sites their kids visit.
❖ More than half the parents claimed they had better Internet knowledge than their children.

❖ Twenty-four percent of teens claimed their parents are never around when they are online; 6 percent of parents claimed they are never around when their children are online.

❖ Seventy-one percent of parents believe their children use the Internet for research, while only 23 percent of teens say they research online.

Signs that your child may be being cyber-bullied

▶ long hours on the computer

▶ secretive about Internet activities

▶ always on the computer but getting behind on homework

▶ won't say who they're talking to

▶ may hide unexplained pictures on the Net

▶ lack of appetite, trouble sleeping, crying for no reason

▶ loss of interest in social events

▶ marked change in attitude or dress

▶ unexplained broken personal possessions, loss of money, etc.

▶ acting out aggression, and

▶ drop in school grades and motivation.

Obviously, any of these symptoms could just be a normal part of growing up, but if many symptoms apply, your child probably needs help.

Teacher says ...

Following a nasty cyber-bullying incident at the high school where I teach, I conducted an anonymous survey. It turned out that nearly every student I asked had shared their Internet/email/MSN password with one or a couple of special friends. They did so to show these friends how special they were, a bit like a blood-brother commitment. This is great, so long as none of these special friendships hits any turbulence ...

A new bag of nasties

Here is a list of the most common online antics, which can cause so much pain.

- ❖ *Signing on with someone else's details* to gain information, post to forums and/or send emails is now a common occurrence. This allows the bully to cloak his identity, and can make innocent parties appear to be the bullies.
- ❖ *IM – the new messaging system.* Instant Messaging – or 'IMing' – is a savvy way of communicating. MSN is just one commonly used program that allows kids to chat to each other online. This form of chatting leads easily to taunts and bullying. Children have the ability to copy conversations and then paste them into emails without others knowing.
- ❖ *Websites.* It is now all too easy to create a web presence. Sites such as MySpace, Facebook, Bebo and YouTube allow children to create a website in minutes and then post onto it photos, sound files and videos, and then broadcast online without permission – around the world!
- ❖ *Internet polls.* Some children go the extreme level of harassment by creating online polls about people they dislike. Children are then invited to register their thoughts, which can be crippling when the target discovers a wave of dislike for him. However, be aware that just one user can vote many times in order to cause much heartache.
- ❖ *Forums and guest books.* Online forums are sites that allow users to post comments in an electronic guest book. When the information posted is defamatory, great pain and upset results.

Teacher says ...

Kids are very resourceful – and they love codes. Parents should look out for any message that says 'POS'. This means 'Parent Over Shoulder'!

Staying safe online

▶ NEVER give out passwords, PINs, etc., even to best friends!

▶ Keep ALL personal information to yourself.

▶ NEVER send a message to someone when you are angry.

▶ Don't stay online all the time – get out of virtual reality and into actual reality.

▶ Don't reply to cyber-bullies.

▶ Don't keep bullying to yourself. Inform your parents, teachers or the local police.

▶ DO NOT DELETE messages from cyber-bullies: www.cyberbullying.ca tells you how to save vital information needed to track them.

▶ Protect yourself – don't privately meet unknown cyber-contacts.

What you can do about cyber-bullying

❖ Don't just rely on filters and believe that your children are safe in cyberspace – parents need to monitor and inform children about the dangers.

❖ Take a strong stand about the time spent in cyberspace. Children need balanced lives, and time and energy spent here mean more potential anxiety and stress, and less time for effective de-stressors such as sport, hobbies and interests, bike-riding, playing with pets, helping out around the home, etc.

❖ Read the riot act to your children about not sharing passwords or PINs.

❖ Perhaps ask the computer teacher at school about educating students about 'Netiquette' and ways to handle cyber-bullying – thereby making students aware that cyber-bullying, which many kids see as fun, is not victimless just because the 'victim' is not present.

Part Five

Home and the school

'... since we can't know what knowledge will be most needed in the future, it is senseless to try to teach it in advance. Instead, we should try to turn out people who love learning so much and learn so well that they will be able to learn whatever needs to be learned.'

John Holt

Schools and home need each other like never before. If we can work together and support each other, we may well produce exciting and viable communities. If we pull apart, our kids and our communities are likely to self-destruct.

This Part covers areas where there is a clear link between home and the school. We will look at food and sleep, so we can all send our kids off to school with enough petrol in the tank to be able to learn. We will ponder that great hot potato, homework, offering some sensible advice and possible directions for learning at home. And this Part will shine a light on the world of technology: our kids are learning in ways we never dreamed possible.

A strong link between home and school allows schools to open their gates and make parents feel part of the school community, just as it allows parents to open their minds and get to know what the teachers are trying to do.

Nutrition for learning

It is vital for children to drink lots of water and have a good diet, not just for physical wellbeing. Parents should consider feeding the brain with more than just questions. Eating oily fish is important for kids. Omega 3 has been shown to build up the myelin sheath coating of the brain's neurons (see the section on the neuron in Appendix II). There is also a wave of support for bananas and frequent sips of water as brain boosters!

Teacher says ...

- Explain to your child not to swap or share her lunch.
- Let the teacher and/or the principal know if your child is allergic to certain foods.
- Check that your child likes the food you are preparing.
- Pack food that is easy to eat – and won't make a mess.
- Use a lunchbox – and check that it fits in the child's bag.
- Include a frozen drink to help keep the food chilled.
- Make sure your child can open the food wrappings – cling wrap can be a toughie for some kids. A lunchbox with different sections is a great idea.
- With fruit, consider how it will look in hours to come after bumps and bashes.

How to pack a punch with a packed lunch

Pack a lunch for your children in two sections. One is for Recess (or 'play lunch'). Some children will eat all their food at Recess. Having two distinct portions in their own wrapping is a good idea. Schools do not permit kids to share their food, so make sure your child knows this. Also, ensure you check about allergic reactions. Schools now have an Anaphylaxis Policy – which means that you should not let your child take along any peanuts or nut products. The days of peanut-butter sandwiches are sadly no longer with us. Most schools will have the old faithful tuckshop or canteen, staffed by faithful mums ... and some dads. Canteens now have government directives to stock foods grouped in two sections – red food and green food. This means foods such as cakes and chips are available only two days a week. Sugar-sweetened drinks are not sold.

A parent says ...

Help make their day more interesting with a bit of lunch-food flair by including the odd cutlet, homemade goodies, a club sandwich, a wrap, or any other healthy but non-melting favourite.

If mornings are chaotic, prepare, wrap and freeze their lunches the night before. That way the goodies are too frozen to eat at playtime but still fresh at lunchtime. Consider making up a whole week's sandwiches once a week, labelling and freezing them, to free up your mornings even more.

Lighten up about lunch

A neighbour loves sharing her problems – with the rest of the street! 'Look what I found in your bag,' she told her son loud enough for us all to hear. 'Your lunch! Don't worry that I got up at 6.30 to make it for you. You wanted cheese sandwiches and you got them. So? And it's not just today's lunch either, there's yesterday's and the day before's. Your stinky bag will soon walk home on its own!'

It's understandable that parents should get stressed about school lunches, and not just because of the wasted effort. Our society spends a lot of energy worrying about food intake, and well it might, given that dieticians tell us that 60 percent of deaths are diet-related!

Lots of kids lose out on lunch – they are too busy, too hot, there are too many other things to do, and lunch is too boring. Some parents just let them buy it, and keep some control by having their say on what the canteen stocks; others will get the kids to make their own, so they make what they'll eat, and they give the kids the money saved as extra pocket money; others deduct $2 for any food made but not eaten. The best lunches contain variety, with some surprises from time to time.

A true tale ... Freddy

Freddy was a fussy eater who particularly avoided his 'apple a day'. In frustration, his father told him that every day he ate his apple, he would be given 20 cents. Now Freddy soon figured out that he could get 20 cents just for dumping his apple in the bin. When one of his friends told on him, his parents decided they would pay by the scalp; Freddy would get 20 cents for each core he brought home. Being a boy of some ingenuity, Freddy worked out that he could still pocket 15 cents per apple by paying 5 cents to a fruit-loving friend to eat it for him.

When this game was discovered, Freddy just stopped even pretend-ing to eat apples again. In desperation, his dad threatened to give him a swipe on the backside with his belt for every uneaten apple. A few weeks later, his father followed an alcoholic stench to nine uneaten apples in Freddy's bag. He had to follow through on his threat.

Freddy is now 30 and still hasn't forgiven his dad for the thrashing – and he still can't eat apples. His father still remembers crying with every swipe. If only Dad:

♦ hadn't tried to enforce something he couldn't police
♦ had consulted a nutrition chart, which would have shown him that there were dozens of excellent alternatives to apples
♦ hadn't become obsessed with the idea that Freddy's survival hung on an apple tree
♦ hadn't made threats from which he either had to back off and look weak, or enforce and feel weak
♦ and Mum had taken notice of what Freddy really ate in a day
– they would have found more variety and nutrition than most of us think our kids eat.

To eat or not to eat ...

▶ If your child often comes home famished, talk to the teacher: most schools supervise the first half of lunchtime, and can keep kids who avoid eating their lunch nearby.

▶ Remember that everyone has a different cycle: some can't eat much breakfast, or lunch, while others don't eat much dinner, so don't fuss if your child's appetite is not ideal. She will not die of starvation.

▶ Restrict after-school eating if it is interfering excessively with your child's lunch or evening meal. Alternately, as kids' appetites tend to peak between 3 p.m. and 4 p.m., maybe allow healthy snack food after school, so when the tummy grumbles, the kids can quaff down some good food.

▶ Eating in front of TV every night is neither good for digestion nor good for a family's emotional health and survival.

> If the kids will only eat junk food, then chances are that they have some behaviour problems, too. That's the only conclusion to be reached after reading Sue Dengate's book *Fed Up*, which looks at the link between problem behaviours in kids and the foods they eat. Dengate claims that children who are irritable, restless, inattentive, moody, or poor sleepers, and who experience eczema, migraines, headaches, stomach problems, bloating, diarrhoea, bed-wetting, reflux, colic or asthma could well be reacting, at least in part, to common foods. Even if the case is overstated, we can't afford to underrate the issue.

The school canteen and healthy eating

Become involved in developing a good-food policy at your school canteen. After consulting experts in the area, we have come to realise just how much a healthy canteen has to offer not just the kids, but the whole school. Healthy canteen advocates point out the following:

- ❖ If schools are serious about their healthy image, they must have healthy canteens.
- ❖ A school canteen is a major takeaway food outlet, with the potential to earn thousands of dollars for the school each year.
- ❖ The workers constitute one of the biggest volunteer workforces in the community.
- ❖ School canteens have clear guidelines on the type of foods they can sell to their students – programs such as 'Management Sense, Food Sense' from Focis provide a practical manual to assist canteen managers with information and recipe ideas to assist in all areas of canteen management.
- ❖ Healthy school canteens can be just as profitable as those serving unhealthy foods – how profitable a canteen is depends on how efficiently it is run, not on how healthy the food is.
- ❖ Many school canteens now offer healthy breakfasts too, because evidence suggests that children perform better in the classroom if they have had a healthy start to the day and don't skip breakfast.

No more bad eating habits

If your child has ongoing unhealthy food cravings, see your family doctor, who may refer your child to a dietician. But if it's just a bad habit, then take up some of these suggestions:

❖ Cut junk food from the shopping list.

❖ Maybe give afternoon commercial TV a miss, as it's a heavy campaigner for junk food.

❖ Keep plenty of healthy snack foods around, including fruit, muesli, yoghurt, carrot sticks, multi-grain or high-fibre bread, etc.

❖ Keep a list for a day or two of everything that is being eaten at home (and at school, if you know), not only to reassure yourself, but as valuable information for any future discussions with a dietician, doctor or with your child.

Teacher says ...

So much of what children eat depends on the fads of their mates at school. Healthy canteens are becoming more prevalent – local area health services have brochures to assist your canteen with ideas to improve their fare. Generally, the teachers we surveyed were of the opinion that families should set a healthy example and only offer healthy food to kids. Other teachers suggested we should worry less, as kids will eat when they need to. We agree with both schools of thought.

Be patient

Many children get quite excited settling into a new environment, and don't eat their food. Don't be too concerned if this happens occasionally – but do talk to the teacher if you find this is becoming common (around three times a week). Things that look fresh in the morning can quickly become pungent and battered by Recess. Also, remember that children love to talk about what they have in their lunchbox; eating the same sandwiches every day can take the fun out of lunchtimes! Sometimes parents pack too much. Children can't get through it all. Try to find a happy medium between what you send and what comes home.

The other vital ingredient: sleep

It amazes teachers that children attend school underslept, with a brain still dozing – or wanting to doze off at the drop of a hat. Learning is exhausting, so kids need to be ready for it. A vital part of this readiness is sleep.

Here's how it breaks down:

* Infants-aged kids should get about 11–12 hours' sleep a night.
* Primary-aged kids, about 10 hours' sleep a night.
* High-school-aged kids, about nine hours' sleep a night.

This is a rule of thumb only – remember to allow for individual differences.

Some kids – the night owls – will always challenge this (and you!). Set a good wind-down time. Children going to bed after playing a video game for over an hour is not ideal. The brain doesn't switch off: this stimulation before sleep will create tired children the following day. Try to have quiet times before settling for rest.

A true tale ... snoring success

Young Toby was baffling us. He was bright and breezy, but had no concentration and was too easily distracted.

Because he was asthmatic and allergy-prone, we sent him back to the expert to see whether the medication might be the monster. The specialist asked Mum to monitor Toby's sleeping that night and then change to a new prescription the next day. Mum dutifully did that and found that during the first night he snored constantly and woke early, but with the new medication Toby breathed easier and slept longer. His teacher couldn't believe the difference in his concentration – he was at last getting adequate air to his brain, and adequate rest for his body.

Allergies, asthma, nasal polyps, adenoids or enlarged tonsils are often the cause of snoring in children. In adults, snoring does have its uses, as researchers have rated it one of the great contraceptives – no matter what the religion. So you should act now if your little snorer is to have any hope of a loving life. As the late novelist Anthony Burgess said, 'Laugh and the world laughs with you, snore and you sleep alone'.

The 'do's and 'don't's of homework

Isn't it strange? Two positive little words, 'home' and 'work', take on a whole new monstrous meaning when combined in the word 'homework'! It's not just the kids who feel the pain, it's parents and teachers, too. Yet in this age of information explosion, there's a real temptation to rely on homework more and more to help kids and teachers keep pace with progress. We view the out-of-school hours as the chance to learn sports, hobbies and skills that schools can't cover.

Too often, homework becomes a dread and a major source of family friction. Just how typical is this scenario:

A frustrated parent is trying to motivate a less-than-excited child to get her homework done. 'Why don't you just get your homework out and get on with it? What could be done in ten minutes takes us two hours, all because you don't get on with it. Every day it's the same damn thing. Why? You know you've got homework, but you'd rather see the whole house upset because you're too selfish to care. Now get it out and do it – and not another peep out of you till it's finished ...'

This pain is very avoidable.

DO ...

- ❖ have a regular homework time
- ❖ provide a set homework space, free of distractions
- ❖ ensure homework is finished before any after-dinner play or television
- ❖ try to get homework over early, or it can become an all-night battle
- ❖ keep an eye on how long it takes: for infants' grades, it should be fun and never take more than 30 minutes; for primary grades, no more than one hour
- ❖ check with the teacher if your child is having problems
- ❖ avoid regularly fighting over homework – keep the issue simple
- ❖ reward fast, efficient homework if your child is a daydreamer
- ❖ be near enough to help and to provide guidance
- ❖ check the homework, but concentrate on noticing good points
- ❖ if there is an error, see if the child can find it first; if not, gently point out the error but avoid criticism, and
- ❖ make your kids feel important and grown up when they are 'home-working'.

DON'T ...

- ❖ do homework for them, or it becomes a life sentence
- ❖ take responsibility for their homework
- ❖ use your help to lift their marks (and your ego)
- ❖ put pressure on them to get top marks all the time, or they will hate the daily threat
- ❖ get conned by 'I'll do it soon' or 'We didn't get any'
- ❖ allow the television to be on during homework
- ❖ allow younger kids without homework to play nearby

- ❖ focus on their failures – they've probably had a day of that already, and
- ❖ use the old 'In my day ...' spiel – remember how much you hated hearing that as a child ...

A true tale ... Matt

Matt's mum had done well at school and, for her, getting good marks was really important. She had wanted to go on to university, but an unplanned pregnancy had cut short the possibility of a promising career. Housework offered her no stimulation.

When Matt began school, she took great delight in helping him learn. She was thrilled with his achievements and merit certificates, and started to push for more – to the point where Matt began to hate doing homework. Why? Because his mum was only happy if he did well, and ranted and raved if he didn't; the merit certificates were really more a mark of *her* success than Matt's. But if the coach does all the work, the child changes from player to pawn. It wasn't until we were able to separate Mum's ambitions from Matt's homework, and re-focus her drive on self-fulfilment, that Matt was able to find his own levels and his own sense of achievement.

Teacher says ...

Teachers want to be told if any kids are struggling with homework. If your child can't do her homework because she doesn't understand the concepts, don't get into an argument trying to teach her. That is the teacher's role, so let him or her know.

What some kids say about homework

(teachers and parents take note!)

'It seems as if teachers give projects just to keep us occupied. Sometimes I put heaps into one and the teacher only writes "Good work" or "Could be neater" or something.'

'Sometimes I think that teachers think you've got nothing else to do in your life except homework and projects. I don't mind a bit of homework, but I also like the ballet and music that I do after school.'

'I don't think we should put names on projects because I reckon the teacher has favourites and they get better marks every time.'

'I hate it when you put a lot of effort into a project and you get it back and it says you didn't answer the question.'

'For most of my projects, the comments on them have been all bad rather than picking out the good points.'

'I hate it when you have a teacher who you don't think likes you very much, and you get a bad mark, and they write things like "Appalling" or "Disgraceful" on it.'

'I'd done this project and I'd done about eight hours' work, and in the long run when I got all my marks back she said it wasn't even worth handing in. That really made me feel pretty bad.'

'It's not fair because Melissa's mummy does all her work for her.'

A true tale ... homework horrors

I hadn't seen Elaine and her son Sean for years, then one day the door flew open and Elaine stormed into my room.

'Don't say a word, just let me play this for you,' she said. Then out comes a ghetto blaster and Elaine presses 'PLAY'. Here's an edited and decibel-reduced transcript:

[Scene: dining room, one ordinary after-school afternoon.]
Mum says to number-two Son: 'Sean, how about you get your homework done?'

'I am, but I can't do everything at once. One minute it's "shut the door", now it's "do your homework".'

'Okay, well shut the door and then come and do your homework.'

'I am shuttin' the door.'

'Shutt-ing the door, Sean.'

'Oh, terrific, shutt-ing the door. Ing, ing, ing, are you happy now I'm shutt-ing the door?'

'Don't speak to me like that. Just do your homework.'

'That's all you can talk about, homework, homework,' Sean screamed as slamming doors decibelled their sympathies onto the microphone.

Mum thumped the STOP button. 'And that goes on every single day – unless it's a project on animals or snakes.'

'I think your son is under stress,' I mumbled, knowing just how he felt.

Sean was behind in reading; in fact schoolwork was as attractive to him as six years of stretch-sewing would be for me. But for every problem there is an environmental quick-ease. We called Sean's teacher, who had no idea of the domestic drama, and homework changed overnight – more animal projects and less formal work, which the teacher (not Mum) checked each day. Mum's job was to set the scene for quiet homework. Now we were making progress!

I rang Mum the other day to get an update and, believe it or not, so far so good. Elaine said Sean was really 'try-ing'.

Dealing with projects and assignments

Projects and assignments are meant to give kids the chance to explore a topic in depth at their 'leisure'. Unfortunately, the reality is generally a far cry from this ideal. Projects are a great idea if they are well explained, if the material is readily available, if the kids are keen to do them, if there has been plenty of notice given, if the kids are well organised, and if there is some in-school progress review to keep the project on the boil. That's a lot of 'if's, and in many cases not all of this happens. The result can be catastrophic or comical, depending on how far you are from the next deadline!

To build good research skills, the bulk of a project should be done at school, where the teacher can help, check progress, share resources and not penalise those kids whose families don't own encyclopedias or whose parents don't want to take over. The key thing to remember is that your child's balsa-wood project will ultimately match up against an engineer parent's cast-bronze exact replica of London Bridge! Little Jake shoving two sticks over a ditch can feel quite robbed when Thomas brings in an elaborately soldered and stress-tested (by his dad!) suspension bridge.

Projects and the Internet

Yes, the Internet is a great place to do research and gather information. However, kids need to be made aware of the difference between copying someone else's work and referencing or acknowledging sources of information. As parents and teachers, we need to carefully set research tasks that involve gathering relevant information and applying original thought to it. It's one thing to be able to locate and copy three pages of information, but to be able to talk about it in relation to local examples, to apply the information to specific problems or meaningful events is another thing again. A useful site for kids wanting to find answers to just about anything is http://www.askforkids.com/.

A true tale ... Kristen

Kristen came home from school one day with the news that every parent dreads: the project was due in that week. Kristen's project was on the products of New Zealand. Her mother phoned another project-paranoid parent, who hinted that there might be books in the town library. Down Mum raced in her lunch break the next day, but a quick check on the faces of all the other glum mums in the library told her that others were also researching products from New Zealand. Fortunately, a local travel agent helped out, so that night, working on the project became a family affair. Big sister was the artist of the family so, for $5 or an all-weekend wear of Kristen's jeans, she did the map and the title page. Mum prepared the notes and Kristen cut out the pictures.

Mum went above and beyond the call of duty here. It was good of her, but she shouldn't make a habit of it in this way.

Computers and learning

Adults worry about kids in the computer age. We all know that computers are the communication medium of now and the future. Kids enjoy computers; and virtually every school now has its own computer bank! But don't forget about good old books: with pictures and print, they can develop imagination, convey feelings, teach and communicate. But so can computers. They can do all those things *and* play games, improve children's Maths, spelling and reading skills, or assist with any school subject, for that matter.

We worry that computer-addicted kids will become social hermits; but so can 'bookworms'. In fact, some research has found that computer competence actually helps to enhance social skills. We recommend that parents support computer use from a young age, as you do any other learning tool, and be a guiding part of the whole experience. Monitor the computer just as you do the TV. Share in its use, strive for balance, and learn together.

Computer games can teach, too

Intuition and the test of time tell us that playing in the sandpit is a very valuable learning experience. Computer 'games' can be viewed in a similar way. What we may see as simple 'games' on the computer are, more often than not, teaching one thing or another – and we're not talking about the shoot-'em-up-style games here at all – so be patient, look hard, and try to see the hidden value in even the simplest games.

If you're on the Internet, take a look at 'The Children's Technology Review' at http://www.childrenssoftware.com/ for valuable information on software suitable for all ages. And use your parental intuition to make judgements about the appropriateness of software for your child.

There is little doubt that the multimedia nature of the computer can make 'drill and kill' routines more fun, encouraging and promoting all sorts of learning and thinking in our children. Use computers wisely to complement the learning activities that concerned parents have always pursued with their children, and don't forget to make time for the sandpit.

Teacher says ...

Many people perceive computers as only for one child at a time. This is a real waste of the resource. Try getting two or more children onto the computer and teach them to take turns. Get an older child to sit with a younger child to 'show' her how to use a program. You will be amazed at how much communication and interaction a computer can lead to.

Safe computer use

There are some general principles that apply to children of most ages:

▶ Involve the kids in developing Internet guidelines that everyone feels are fair and reasonable (and is therefore more likely to accept and follow).

▶ Take an interest in new sites children find online, and spend time exploring with them.

▶ Keep in touch with what the kids are doing online.

▶ Put the computer(s) with Internet access in a public area of the home rather than in a child's bedroom.

▶ Have family talks about the Internet, and encourage your children to let you know if they come across anything disturbing.

▶ Discuss the nature of material found on the Internet rather than just acting as chief censor. Your kids need to know what your values are and why you have strong feelings about offensive material.

The Internet has really come of age. It is like an endless bookstore with attitude. There are all sorts of people and things in places around the world that you do and don't want to interact with. The trick is to learn how to use it effectively. We're not suggesting that you get your three-year-old online as soon as possible, but merely that you don't turn your back on this tool because it's 'too hard' or dangerous. The Internet is a fact of life, like TV and telephones, and your children are better off learning about it at home with you than anywhere else.

A true tale ... Jason, the computer nerd

Jason was a computer nerd. He loved machines but just couldn't handle people. If any teacher had a go at him, he'd foul-mouth his way into one school suspension after another. We'd tried relaxation, we'd tried getting him to zip his mouth when he felt the temper rising, but in the heat of the action this failed every time.

We realised we were asking a social misfit to be socially clever; we were ignoring his 'hotspot'. If computers were where his head was, that's where we had to be. Jason said that if he wanted to stop the action on his computer, he would click on the word 'Suspend'. After practising being teased and getting ruffled, Jason was prepared mentally to click on 'Suspend' and ignore all provocation until he felt back in balance: so far so good! This may not be a perfect solution, but using 'Suspend' is one heck of a lot better than being 'suspended'. The best way to help kids is to use their strength rather than pick on their weakness.

Teacher says ...

If children become obsessed by computer games, put a timer on and stick to it. Any complaints, and their computer time is lost. If arguments persist, switch it off and give them time to dry out, get out(doors) and help out!

Juggling work and school support

Overworked parents can be over-wound, over-used, and have little time to relax and recover. The very thing that the extra work was meant to provide, a happy family, disappears into the mist of the materialism myth.

The majority of the mothers and fathers of primary-aged children are in the workforce. Many mothers are particularly sensitive about the impact of this work commitment on their children, but there is no research – to our knowledge – suggesting that, if the situation is well handled, the children should be disadvantaged in any appreciable way.

But it's not easy. There's the daily rush of getting up early to get the kids dressed and breakfasted, their hair done and teeth cleaned, organise the lunches, hang the washing, tidy the house and deposit the children in time to enjoy a good traffic snarl before a day's work. Then it's back home to take in the washing, cook dinner, clean up, handle the homework, and iron out whoever or whatever has any wrinkles. No wonder the wheels fall off at weekends.

Assuming, as is the case in almost all families, that Mother is the domestic coordinator, we need to share responsibilities. As a general rule, children do better and feel better if Dad (or someone other than Mum) is involved in their schoolwork and homework. We strongly recommend that fathers, even if shift-workers, pilots or weekend dads, become the key school-support person. This doesn't mean Dad downs tools and races off to school over every issue, but that he becomes the parental point of contact. Kids benefit, mums get relief, and relationships between fathers and family are strengthened.

Let's stop the 'Dad drift'

In a study, little kids drew family pictures with Dad in close, but nine- to twelve-year-olds drew Dad as more distant, and surrounded by material goods such as boat, car or surfboard. Children's self-esteem can be strongly influenced by how often they see their dads. As Professor Don Edgar says, 'If a father's not there, it's like driving on two cylinders instead of four.'

Teacher says ...

It's sad to see so many parents in such a hurry that they show little interest in what their child may have made or done during the day. Often we see the children just so excited to show off their art, and Mum will say, 'Hmm, lovely', then put it in the bin on the way out. In time, I believe those children won't want to produce their best or be proud of their work – and then the parents will complain that their kids are lazy and don't try.

A true tale ... Stevie

Stevie looked up to his father almost as if he were a god. The irony of this was that his dad *was* somewhat of a god – a vision that fleetingly passed in and out of Stevie's life but never really touched him. In therapy, Stevie's father was adamant that he was an excellent provider. Stevie had the latest baseball jacket and top-of-the-range running shoes. Dad had made good his promise that his kids would never be 'without' in the way he had been as a child. Only the emotional care and stability Stevie required, as a difficult child, was never provided.

Stevie's dad retired several years later and became a volunteer worker and financial backer for a youth support scheme. But by then it was too late for Stevie. As someone once said, our kids would be much richer if we spent half as much money on them and twice as much time.

Top tips: What you can do

➡ Financial concerns can destroy marriages if they are allowed to become the top priority. Your family is your biggest investment, so it's worth getting it right!

➡ If you are often at work, try to organise one regular, warm, cosy, loving, special babysitter. Grandparents are often eager, but we caution against using them too regularly, as it can cause resentment either when they want a break or if they start to take over.

➡ Try not to have your kids going to multiple carers in one day (before school, preschool, after school, etc.) – that requires too many adjustments to be made to too many people. While it might suit your career, we find some kids become very stressed and distressed and, as a result, become very difficult little customers when parents do take over. Kids need down-time, lap-time, cuddle-time, play-time ... our time.

➡ If you have primary-school-aged children and you can't always be home with them after school, make sure they have some company. For high-schoolers who come home alone by choice, consider getting a pet to provide company, leaving friendly messages around, or phoning from work.

Change gears between work and home

Some parents arrive home still in full work mode. We suggest you do some 'decomposing' as follows:

❖ On your way home, change mental gear.

❖ Before you hit the front door, project beyond that door to what might be happening on the other side (kids fighting, wanting homework help, competing for your attention, dobbing and counter-dobbing, etc.).

❖ Don't touch the phone, computer or mail for the first half-hour. Be with your family.

A true tale ... tag parenting

Jeff was a working dad and Anne was a working night nurse. They had two preschool kids. Dad would do the washing, get them up and off in the morning, and then in the afternoon Anne would collect, bath and feed them, get the washing in, wash up and prepare breakfast, then 'tag' Jeff as he walked in, and off she'd go on night duty. Jeff would do the getting-to-bed-routine.

It's called tag parenting, and it's okay in theory, but can create big problems in practice. If you must have a tag turnover, then try to keep the routines consistent. Take time just for each other and, for the parent racing home to cover the kids, do some unwinding on the way: before you hit home, think positively about the kids in order to be ready, so that the shock to the system doesn't emotionally electrocute the whole family. It's a bit sad, in a way, that the romantic touch that made us parents has turned into the tired touch of a tagging twosome. As some cynic said, unless we take stock, home will soon be merely the place part of the family waits till the rest of the family brings the car back.

Family life is certainly not what it was in the olden days. So much to do, so little time ... but remember this: your children won't remember how much you did for them, they will remember how you felt along the way. As Ogden Nash said, progress may have been all right once, but it has gone on for far too long.

Part Six

Trouble-shooting

'... the biggest lesson you can learn in life, or teach your children, is that life is not castles in the skies, happily ever after. The biggest lesson we have to give our children is truth.'

Goldie Hawn

Thriving at school means overcoming problems. We are suggesting that parents play a greater role in their kids' schooling, so we have to accept that the learning journey will hit some speed humps from time to time. This Part deals with some of the 'troubles' you may encounter. Troubles are  truths – allow your child to experience the truth rather than 'fixing' or 'hiding' it. Troubles do happen – that's life.

Possible school 'troubles' include attendance, home-schooling, academic reports, complaints, interviews, discipline matters and school excursions. These are the issues on which parents and schools come together, and hopefully interact rather than impact! The stronger the home–school link, and the more families and schools work together on these and all other issues, the more successful we will be in having kids who thrive at school.

Absenteeism and 'school sickness'

Absenteeism from school is a major problem. Not only does frequent absence mean that kids won't reach their potential, and reduces their academic confidence, it can also reduce their social confidence, as they aren't at school to nourish their friendships.

There are five common factors behind poor attendance:

1 *Family background* – poor housing, uninterested parents, criminal activity, parent separation or absence, many siblings, etc.

2 *Academic difficulties* – special needs not being recognised or catered for, language problems, etc.

3 *Relationship problems* – a personality clash with the teacher, being bullied or bullying (and unpopular), a misfit in class, separation anxiety from parent, unable to relate to peers, etc.

4 *Behavioural difficulties* – reaction to home problems, hyperactivity, school phobia, anxiety, psychiatric problems, aggressiveness, stubbornness, etc.

5 *School-based problems* – ineffective monitoring, poor welfare system, poor home/school liaison, lack of relevance in the curriculum, unawareness by staff of student need, etc.

On average, at least one child in every primary class is away each day with what is termed 'parent-condoned absenteeism'.

During the school day, the safest place for children is at school. Students of all ages are less likely to become targets or perpetrators of crime if they are at school. Parents play a key role in this. The best way to prevent major attendance problems is to have a home policy that says, if it's a school day and the kids are not sick, they go to school.

Are they really sick?

The problem for many parents is to know whether the kids are really sick or 'school sick' (i.e. faking it). Head and tummy ailments are the clear favourites, but some of the more creative reasons include: being unable to stand, blurred vision, the recurrence of an earache 'only worser', red-pen-looking spots on the tummy, and writer's cramp. One child even claimed a premonition of a bomb threat! Parent explanations are just as comical – 'She's got a cartridge in her knee', 'He suffers from a genital bad back', 'She had to go back to the doctor's for her leg', 'She hates going and has become an electric newt' (elective mute), 'His father was home', 'Couldn't wake the bugger', and 'Please excuse my child as she was absent'.

If your child often feels sick before school, or if the recovery rate after 9 a.m. is truly remarkable, it's worth looking for outside causes such as too many late nights, too much junk food, or just too much else on. Maybe 'taking sickies' is a family virus, or perhaps the child is failing in the playground or the classroom. An ounce of prevention is worth a pound of cure, so try a balanced diet, a balanced life, some time to talk about any problems, and a general drop in home bustle and bristle. If a happier, problem-free home doesn't help, then talk to the teacher or counsellor and get some school or remedial help.

'School sickness' checklist

- Is there a medical reason for it?
- Does the sickness happen every morning or just on school days?
- Does the child get miraculously better after 9 a.m.?
- Has the teacher indicated that the child was ill at school?
- Does the sickness happen at particular times – for example, when the child gets up or gets dressed?
- Are there more tears than are normally associated with an illness?
- Is there more anger than sadness if the child is forced to go to school? (Anger can indicate that something else is underpinning the 'sickness'.)
- Does it seem to make a difference who takes the child to school?
- Are there other emotional indicators that it's 'school sickness', such as more nightmares, a loss of energy, the child becoming clingy, etc.?

'School sick' or school phobia?

School phobia is not a case of 'school sickness'. It's not just a fear of going to school; it makes attendance a downright impossibility. There are other important differences, too: there may be no physical complaints (although nausea, headaches and tummy aches are nearly always present), and generally school phobia is more a fear of leaving home than a fear of going to school. The other big difference is in degree. Usually kids with 'school fear' can be coaxed along or offered an incentive to get them under way: their resistance is frequently more symbolic than real. With children suffering from school phobia, the fear is quite frantic, and their resistance to school is extreme to the point of being dangerous.

The reasons why such a phobia develops are many and varied. In every such case, the child has been a worrier who swallowed his or her anxieties. But as about half the population (including adults!) can be classified as 'internalisers', this alone is not a sufficient explanation. Frequently, a child with school phobia may have experienced some trauma associated with going to school or leaving home. The trauma triggers include a parent disappearing from the family while the child was at school; something nasty happening on the way to school; being assaulted or hounded by a bully at school; soiling or wetting their pants at school; parents splitting up or arguing a lot; a parent who is depressed and upset; some form of suicidal talk within the family; and a death in the family.

Children with school phobia are at real risk, and need quick, clever and professional help. Whatever you do, don't try forcing phobic kids out of their 'silly' behaviour.

A true tale ... Angela

Angela was a bright and high-spirited nine-year-old who excelled at school. Mum was an artist and, since her separation, had been away from home more than she would have liked, to do business, exhibit her work, etc. Angela started to get mystery illnesses that kept her home from school. At first, a guilt-ridden Mum dropped everything and tried to stay home with her until she was better, but doctors could never find any real cause. Mum started to realise that it was all in Angela's mind, so she tried forcing her to school. Angela would hold on to the car seatbelt or the door, pull Mum's hair and scream if anyone tried to force her out of the car. Angela got on well with Mum's sister, so we ended up telling Mum to take her to Aunty's place, leave her there, get on with her business, come back there for bed and breakfast, and then take off for work the next day.

Mum did this for just three days. Angela found she could survive without Mum but she missed her friends. Mum stayed home more, took a hard line, and hasn't had any trouble since. Sometimes, the more severe the problem, the smarter the cure needs to be.

Top tips: what you can do

➤ If the problem is serious, get professional help from a clinical child psychologist or the school counsellor.

➤ Don't expect that logical, rational means will sort the problem out – school phobia is not a rational problem! Children can promise to go the next day and mean it, but when faced with the reality, their wish is no match for their fear. They might know their terror is silly, but they can't do a thing about it.

➤ Don't tell school-phobic kids how to beat their phobia, let them see and feel success. This means helping them reach very small goals at first, so small that they almost stumble over success without trying. Small goals may be as elementary as walking past the school, putting the uniform on, or just walking down the street. It's important to start small and build from there.

➤ Don't let your children's fears, or their capacity to make you feel you are to blame, push you into a corner. Don't bend over backwards to make them happy when the real problem is that they are sinking fast and are using excuses to hide their fear.

➤ Any staying at home on school days has to be as uninteresting as possible, so that time off from school isn't attractive. This means no television, eating play-lunch and lunch at the same time as they would at school, no snacks, no computer time and, if Mum and/or Dad had plans to go out, that's what you do, so long as arrangements have been made for someone to keep an eye on things back home.

Teacher says ...

If you think your child's malingering, send him to school – teachers will call you if the sickness is real. Teacher, counsellor and home must work together on problems of school resistance. As one teacher said, 'Give school-sick children a dose of cod-liver oil – it's good for them and will soon sort out the sick from the pseudo-sick.'

What not to do

- Don't make outside appointments for your child during school hours if he has a chequered attendance history.
- Don't allow kids to stay home on sport days – sport is an important part of a child's development. Find a sport that suits their build, talents, preferences and personality.
- Don't give your kids a day off just in case they're sick – instead, give the school a contact phone number if needed.
- If they convince you they are genuinely sick and must stay at home, don't allow them to run around and have free time – put them to bed.
- Don't allow them out of the house even after school – if they're too sick for school, then they're too sick for play.
- Don't take family holidays during term if possible (especially if the kids have a history of school aversion), as it makes attendance harder upon your return.
- Don't deny the possibility of a school problem; make a fairly fast appointment to talk to the teacher.
- If the fear is not easing, consult a counsellor or clinical psychologist.

'Mondayitis' – what to do

Children love role-play ... and parents are the greatest real-life studies. So when you wake up and feel that sinking, 'back to work' Monday moment, don't act it out in front of the kids. If you do, you will soon also be on the receiving end of some good acting. If children are showing signs of illness, track the days they are sick. If the same day recurs, ask questions – it could be a school-related 'illness'.

What about time off during the term?

Schools require a written request and an explanation for taking any extended leave during term time. Most schools understand the benefits of a one-off holiday, but would advise against frequent breaks. Children need routines – they thrive on consistency. This boosts their confidence for learning, and ensures they are not missing out on anything important.

Handling complaints about school

When your child comes home with a school-related problem, how you deal with it is of paramount importance. It is all too easy to jump to the child's defence. Your prodigy is very accurate in his perspective – he knows it happened 'just like that'. But there are always two sides. And when you discover that your Gentle Jai is really Giant Jai, the playground stand-over man, it can be very humbling!

The best advice is not to interrogate – or even interview. Better to just acknowledge the concern briefly and move onto another subject. If it's an ongoing problem, arrange an interview with the teacher to discuss the matter politely.

Avoid the 'carpark committees'

When your child comes home with a difficulty, it is all too easy to communicate that issue to other mums and dads. This can have a negative effect, causing the issue to become a problem.

All schools have 'carpark committees'. They hold daily meetings, and the agendas are usually set around 'problems'. To ensure there is a mutual support between teachers and parents, it is important that you first talk to the teacher, who will have information from the coalface rather than the carpark.

There will inevitably be issues as your child spends 13 years of his development at school! Deal with problems promptly.

What about changing schools?

If you make a choice of a school and it doesn't seem to be working out for whatever reason, don't be hasty in making a change. Talk with your child's teacher, the school principal and counsellor first; if changing still seems necessary, look for a natural break – the school holidays, the end of a school year – to make the change.

A true tale ... Andrew changing school

Mr and Mrs Newton had separated, but they didn't want that to affect their child's education. So they took Andrew with them to several private and public schools, then asked him which one he thought would be best for his education. He chose the one they least liked. When they asked him why he had chosen that particular school, he said that he really liked the food smells coming from the canteen they passed on the way to the office.

Sometimes we ask children to make decisions on things way beyond their scope or experience.

Academic reports

One aspect of education that hasn't changed is the 'school report', issued twice a year. In many ways it is still the time of reckoning, although the modern report is much more 'receiver-friendly' and tries to be constructive.

Many changes have occurred in the reporting process of late. Now many teachers are given a choice of recommended terms, to cushion hard messages with a soft, sanitised landing. The sanitisation of comments can be taken to the extreme. Here's one parent's interpretation of these politically correct terms:

Recommended term	Translation
Writing 'writes independently' 'writes creatively' 'uninhibited in writing'	leader in illicit note-growing no resemblance to Queen's English responsible for toilet graffiti
Drama 'enjoys acting' 'works expertly in mime'	he's the class clown imitates me behind my back
Listening 'listens creatively' 'listens with open mind' 'listens intermittently'	answers never match the question open to every distraction sometimes hears the bell
Reading 'reads maturely' 'can recognise words' 'sound library skills' 'confident speller'	check under his bed as being distinct from pictures can never find him at lunchtime ignores his mistakes
Mathematics 'shows Maths insight' 'knows basic processes'	beyond anything we can figure just can't apply them

Recommended term	Translation
Language	
'argues forcibly'	won't take no for an answer
'concise in discussions'	yes, no, shrug are his repertoire
'participates well in discussions'	never shuts up
General comments	
'likes a structured program'	needs institutionalising
'has an inquiring mind'	can never find him
'enjoys extracurricular activities'	is a delinquent
'tries hard'	is thick as two planks
'has talent'	both planks are warped
'must apply more effort'	is bone lazy
'has trouble concentrating'	is off with the fairies
'good exam result'	must have cheated
'a pleasing report'	didn't know this child existed

While this is clearly tongue-in-cheek, many of the report forms have become so vague that they are vacuous, and so complex that they are confusing. Regardless of format, parents who are in touch with their children's schooling should get few surprises at report time; if you are shocked or disappointed, start a dialogue with the class teacher. More can be discovered via open conversation than written reports.

Consider Winston Churchill's report card from 1883:

- ❖ Eighth out of eleven in Composition, Grammar and Diligence: Composition – very variable; Grammar – fair; Diligence – very naughty.
- ❖ Seventh out of ten in Maths and French – not very good.
- ❖ Weak in Geography
- ❖ Drawing – very elementary.

Responding to reports

▶ If you are going to be critical, be careful. One student approached his father with his report and another that was old and dusty. 'Here's my report, Dad,' he said, 'and here's an old one of yours I found in the attic ...'

▶ The secret is to check the report for comments about the child's effort at school rather than just grades. If the remarks about effort are okay, then school is okay, and the child has done his best. The rest is really a matter of fine-tuning and steering. A tutor can help if the grades are down a bit; the teacher should be contacted if the grades are disastrous.

▶ If the child's efforts at school are not very good, it is essential to hunt for explanations. You can make children physically attend school but you can't force their minds to obey – motivation is the message.

▶ If the report is disappointing, sit down with your child and ask him to identify the areas causing most difficulty. Let him predict where he thinks he can improve. Together, work out how this improvement can be achieved and pencil this in on the report for reference at the next report time. You could formulate set times to work, change priorities or hire a tutor – anything that will help your child taste success and applause (because these things are the big motivators), not punishment.

▶ If the conversation becomes very tense, contact the school counsellor or the school learning-support team as soon as possible for help.

Handling the interview about a bad report

When you think about it, children will have good years, better years and not-so-good years – that's life. Even the not-so-good years academically can be real winners if the kids feel good about school, do well in sport or music or in some other interest area. Kids never progress in a straight line. A good report should highlight strengths as well as weaknesses. Come at any weakness by first focusing on your child's strength. As we know about thriving as a learner, values, attitudes and habits are the keys to success. It is important we don't allow a report to cripple a love of learning.

Many schools now have student-led conferences, whereby the student, in front of parent and teacher, talks about the report and his progress and makes suggestions as to where and how he intends to improve. Although it's more exhausting for everyone, it puts responsibility for learning where it belongs: on the learner.

Teacher says ...

■ No parent or child should receive a shock report if teachers communicate regularly. If parents consult teachers regularly, attend interviews and parent–teacher nights, the report will be more of a summary than a judgement.

■ Before the report comes home, perhaps ask the student to write his own report, which can then be discussed against the teacher's version.

Ten commandments for parents' educational salvation

1 Parents shall honour each other (if more than one exists) and shall honour the school if they expect their children to honour them.

2 Parents shall model good behaviour if they expect good behaviour from their kids – good behaviour by kids is more caught than taught.

3 Parents shall say good things to other adults about their kids while in their hearing – what adults say to each other about kids has a profound effect on their behaviour (good and bad) and on their self-image.

4 Parents shall not overreact to children's successes or failures, or the kids will come to fear the pressure to succeed and will feel despair in failure.

5 Parents shall remember that self-confidence in kids is developed not through indulgence, but through challenge – so don't make the path too smooth or they'll slip.

6 Parents shall remember that children must crawl before they walk – hand over the reins steadily and gradually over time so they develop confidence and self-control.

7 Remember that any family that is divided against itself or against the school will have children divided against authority.

8 Parents shall not invoke confrontations with children unless parents are able to manage the outcomes.

9 Parents shall not protect their children from all forms of competition – competition is one important way children learn to achieve, but over-competitiveness is one sure way for kids to forever feel inadequate.

10 Parents shall work hard to show how learning connects with living if they want their children to view learning as living.

Adapted from some of Sylvia Rimm's 'Laws' (see 'Authors' notes')
and including others of our own.

The ten worst parental sins

'What are the ten worst sins a parent can commit in the schooling of their kids?' We put that question to hundreds of teachers, and here are their answers (with the worst sin last):

10 POOR DIET – many teachers complained that kids come to school with no breakfast, and chips for lunch, and then are edgy and irritable all day.

9 SIBLING COMPARISON – many parents expect their child to perform as well as a sibling; this is dangerous and damaging.

8 NOT ENFORCING SCHOOL ATTENDANCE – not only does this make it harder when kids have to go, they also lose contact with other kids and confidence in their work.

7 FREQUENT CHANGE OF SCHOOL – this caused kids to lose confidence in school and in themselves because they couldn't establish a secure friendship group.

6 NOT READING TO KIDS – reading to kids not only gives them a love of listening to words and stimulates their imagination, it also provides important cuddle-time between parent and child.

5 PUTTING DOWN THE TEACHER OR THE SCHOOL – the effect of this is much the same as parents putting each other down: kids are caught with split loyalties.

4 LACK OF CONSISTENCY – kids will not become well disciplined if the rules are not consistent.

3 PARENTS BEING EDUCATIONALLY UNCARING – parents who take no interest in school tend to breed kids with similar attitudes.

2 LACK OF DISCIPLINE – kids cannot feel confident and secure if the rules are 'wishy-washy'.

1 PARENTS NOT CARING ABOUT THEIR KIDS – by far the biggest sin is the devastating effect of parents just not caring about their kids.

Dealing with teachers

School is part of life, and kids have to learn to cope with the good, the bad and the ugly. Let us make it quite clear that we do not help our kids one bit by torpedoing their teachers. Education is a joint effort; you can't sink one end of the boat and expect the other to keep afloat. Your child has to cope day in and day out with that imperfect teacher, and that teacher has to cope with your imperfect child.

❖ If your child has a problem with most teachers, then if it's not an authority problem, it could well be a cover for the fact that he is not coping with the schoolwork, so spend your energy on that problem, not on confronting the teacher.

❖ Don't take sides with either the child or the teacher – that just makes things worse. Give them time to adjust to each other.

❖ If you want to talk about a teacher with your partner, wait until the kids are safely asleep. There are two reasons for this. First, the children have to go on working with and relating to the 'ogre' you are unhappy with. Second, kids have big ears – they love having news that will be attention-grabbing at school, so they will freely air your secrets as a means of boosting their ego.

There could be many reasons for a teacher to give you or your child a bad impression that have nothing to do with disliking your child. Friendly communication is the best way to prevent little problems reaching paranoid proportions.

Interviews with teachers

Parents are often nervous about seeing their children's teachers. If there is a problem, either with the child or the teacher, here are some strategies to make the most of the opportunity:

▶ Find out when the teacher is available to see parents. Try to arrange a time when the teacher won't be distracted by other kids; see them, for example, after school or during 'release' time.

▶ Talk it over at home with your child and your partner but, at this stage, don't make any accusations, just gather facts.

▶ Write out your questions, and gear them towards solving the problem (e.g. 'What would you suggest ... ?').

▶ Try to keep the focus on the child and the current problem. Raising an old problem from a previous year is usually counter-productive.

▶ Express your views confidently – let's face it, no-one knows your child better than you, and the aim of most interviews is to help all the parties get to know each other as real people, not just as student, teacher or parent.

▶ Try to direct the discussion towards steps that can be taken to improve the situation so that everyone will know what they are aiming for. Sum up and make another meeting time to review progress.

It's worth remembering that *kids are the guaranteed losers in any conflict between the school and the home.*

Does the teacher dislike my child?

Symptom	Other possible reason
Homework not marked.	Work hasn't been handed in; crisis in teacher's home.
Child kept in to finish work.	Your child needs extra time to work, as he doesn't finish class work or homework.
Teacher always yelling.	Teacher yells at everyone.
Child comes home crying.	Other kids are giving him a bad time; having problems with schoolwork; feels unwell.
Child hates school.	Child can't keep up but won't admit it; is being bullied but won't tell.
School reports are bad.	Child is falling behind, so misbehaves.
Child's work has deteriorated.	Teacher is uninspiring; child is unwell.
Child no longer tries.	Child is being nagged; feels he is failing; family expectations are out of his educational reach.
Child is always in trouble for talking, distracting others or not concentrating.	Social needs may outweigh educational needs; child has an attention-deficit difficulty.
Did better in younger grades.	Child is losing heart with harder work – a good home can give a head-start, but that sometimes dissipates over time.
Teacher is always cranky.	The teacher has teenagers, is getting divorced, has missed a promotion, wants to leave teaching but there are no other jobs, is renovating, feels ostracised by the other staff, can't manage discipline easily, can't cope with noise, is poorly organised or is overstressed generally.
Child's grades have dropped.	Different grading styles, e.g. this teacher may not give marks for decoration or good colouring-in.

A true tale ... the great debate

This teacher, who was a bit of a bully, ran the debating team and imagined himself as a super sleuth. He was putting a Year 6 boy through his paces.

'Pick that piece of paper up, son.'

'But sir, my mate said that you dropped it.'

'Oh, so you believe you can really trust your mates, do you?'

'Yes sir, absolutely.'

' "Absolutely"?' repeated the teacher, looking around at the crowd that had gathered. 'Tell me son, do you have a locker?'

'Yes, sir, I do.'

'Do you have a lock on that locker?' the teacher asked as he again turned to the crowd.

'Yes sir, I do.'

'Well,' said the teacher, 'if you trusted your so-called mates absolutely, why, my boy, do you keep a lock on the locker?' He grinned again, looking to the crowd for approval.

Quick as a flash, the boy replied, 'Uh, well, you see, sir, teachers also walk past that area.'

A red-faced teacher ordered the boy up to the office and away from the cheering crowd.

Complaining about a teacher

At some time during your child's education, you will be unhappy with something a particular teacher does or says, or with the style of teaching. If you need to lodge a complaint, here are some guidelines:

Do	Don't
Know your facts.	Listen to hearsay or rumour, or assume your child's version of events is correct on every occasion.
Try to resolve the issue with the teacher in the first instance.	Write to the local authorities or politicians as a first step.
Approach the school in a courteous manner.	Threaten school staff, yell or abuse in any way.
Keep it focused on the issue and be specific.	Generalise about the teacher or school in a negative manner – that will only make the school defensive and take the discussion off-course.
Think about possible solutions to resolve the issue. These should be reasonable, achievable and realistic.	Demand one solution (e.g. move your child to another class) as that may not be possible, and then there's nothing left to negotiate.
Listen to the teacher's and/or the principal's account and explanation.	Assume your child has all the facts and no other explanation is possible.
Try to reach agreement or resolution even if it is a compromise.	Be totally inflexible.
Put the issue behind you once resolved.	Keep harassing the family and school over it.

Real grievances, if well handled and well resolved, build respect between home and school. But if parents are on a vendetta and determined to bring the teacher or the school to their knees, it is very difficult to find resolution, and the message presented to the child can be counter-productive. As we discussed in Part Two, our values and our attitudes are key elements in thriving as a learner.

A true tale ... Ryan – the law of averages

Ryan had just had two super teachers, but his teacher in Year 3 just didn't rate in comparison. His parents noticed his enthusiasm for school was heading downhill fast, and it came to a head when his dad went to pick Ryan up from school and heard the teacher bawling him out at the top of her voice.

Dad's first impulse was to go in and give teacher a bit of the same medicine, but he knew that that would help no-one. Instead, Ryan's parents asked for an interview and discovered that the teacher was well aware of the problem, but felt she just couldn't match her predecessors. This admission was all that was needed; after that, Ryan agreed that the teacher needed help in getting to know him, so one day he took in his car collection to show her, and special drawings on another day.

In time, Ryan and the teacher began to understand each other much better. Before long, the teacher noticed a change that had started to snowball. Ryan was up and running again – all because the teacher was honest and the parents were open enough to listen before they leapt.

Discipline, rights and responsibilities

A headmaster told us that parents believe discipline to be a wonderful thing – when it involves other parents' children. Virtually every school now has a behaviour code. It doesn't rely on the cane, it doesn't rely on hurting kids, it relies on *teaching* kids. It relies on consensus, consistency and firm consequences.

Kids today are quick to assert their rights – we have to link these to responsibilities. Discipline can foster positive attitudes and can get children back on track. And having the 3Rs – Respect, Responsibility and Relationships – as well as positive attitudes, is the key to thriving as a learner.

If we are seeking to promote greater responsibility, and nurture *self-discipline*, it is really important that we get kids involved in the rule-making for the school world in which they live. Good schools have developed a behaviour code in conjunction with parents, teachers and pupils so that the whole school community has some ownership of and allegiance to it – it's their code. Likewise, every school system should have developed well-documented and objective criteria and procedures for serious breaches of that behaviour code. But be aware that issues involving different learners are never black and white. There are always some things that just don't seem fair to one party, while to the other party involved, the action may seem very fair!

Here is one school's code of rights and responsibilities.

Rights	Responsibilities
To be treated with dignity and respect.	To treat staff, students and visitors with consideration and respect. To respect the rights of others to work free of distractions. To move around the school in an appropriate manner. To display behaviour which, at the school and in public, bring credit to oneself and the school. To wear the school uniform correctly and with pride.
To feel secure in an environment free from negative actions from others and from harmful substances and objects.	Not to bring to school substances which are harmful to health and items which have the potential to cause injury. Not to hurt or cause harm to others. To contribute your best efforts. To help keep classrooms tidy. To respect school grounds and property.
To study, work and pursue activities in pleasant, well-kept surroundings.	To eat and drink outside classroom blocks, the library building, etc. To remain within school boundaries. To dispose of litter in the bins provided. To not bring chewing gum to school.
To have belongings treated with care.	To respect the belongings of others. To use personal electronic equipment in such a way that it does not offend, impede learning opportunities, or cause distraction.
To be communicated with clearly, politely and respectfully.	To communicate with others clearly, politely and respectfully.
To have viewpoints and contributions respected.	To treat the viewpoints of others with respect. To respect the ethos and values that underpin our school.

Suspensions and expulsions

Parents who are in regular contact with the school through canteen work, the uniform pool, parent groups, working bees, or as a parent helper, etc. will know early in the piece if problems are occurring, and can prevent them escalating to the point of expulsion or suspension.

However, if you do get the dreaded phone call that tells you your child's services are no longer required, you can generally assume there has been either a long track-record of problems, a violent episode, or some other very serious breach of the code for this decision to be made.

On the whole, it is probably unwise to try and handle this on your own. If your child is heading for suspension, consult the school counsellor or guidance officer and seek outside professional help and advice. When you attend the school interview, try to avoid any confrontation or attribution of blame; keep the focus on the problems and the plan of action suggested to solve them. If there has been some recent change in family health or circumstances, ensure the school is made aware of this, because it might explain the child's behaviour and may convince the school to let him stay on while everything settles down. If the problem is a long-standing one, get a full medical and psychological assessment of your child. After the suspension has been settled, work out what is expected and who will be checking that the strategies are working.

The principles behind suspension

▶ All students have the right to be treated fairly and with dignity in an environment free from disruption, intimidation, harassment and discrimination.

▶ There will be cases where a student's behaviour requires suspension or expulsion.

▶ Parents and the school community should be aware of the procedures.

▶ Suspension is most effective when it highlights the parent's or caregiver's role in collaborating with the school to change the student's behaviour so that the student can rejoin the school community as quickly as possible.

▶ Suspension also allows students time to reflect on their behaviour and to accept responsibility to change their behaviour to meet the school's expectations. It also allows time for school personnel to plan appropriate support to assist with a successful re-entry.

Top tips: what you can do

➠ Leap into action straight away if the warning signs are becoming ominous. Set up a time to meet the principal and arrange regular meetings thereafter to review your child's progress.

➠ Do assume that your child has a problem. Parents who defend and excuse their kids for serious behaviour problems aren't doing their kids one bit of good. These kids never learn to take responsibility for their own actions, and our prison populations are living testimony to the consequences of that approach.

➠ Before you develop an angry outlook on the suspension or expulsion, take a critical look at yourself to see whether the kids are copying aggressive or antisocial behaviour. They may not be bad kids, just good apprentices.

➠ Let the teacher and the principal know if there have been any dramatic changes in family circumstances that might explain behaviour, particularly if it is out of character.

➠ If your child is to be suspended, then ask for the action to be confirmed in writing. Make sure that the reasons and length of suspension are indicated.

➠ Find out first-hand what conditions need to be met before your child can return to school. This should occur during an interview in which home and school can hopefully agree on what has to be done and who can help the family.

➠ Seek an independent opinion (e.g. from a child psychologist) on the problem if the situation has reached flashpoint.

➠ Ask about other resources, such as special classes for behaviourally disordered children, for slow learners, or for whatever the problem is. There are also specialist teachers for children with behaviour problems in most education departments, to help both the children and the teachers in their management.

A true tale ... 'Buddy'

'Buddy' had been so nicknamed because he was everybody's friend. Even though he had always been a bit of a handful, his parents never really believed he was particularly bad. They always claimed he was pretty well behaved at home. And Buddy was a good sportsman, just like his dad.

When Buddy was suspended, his father hit the roof and, after threatening Buddy, decided he'd go and sort the school out. When we became involved, everything was at flashpoint and accusations were being fired in any and every direction. Buddy had committed a few school crimes, the school had been a little lax about informing his parents, and Dad was really offside with the school.

A case conference was set up with the local guidance officer to work out some solutions. The school agreed to write in Buddy's diary every week, and he was given a behaviour card, which his father had to sign daily. A few incentives for good behaviour were set up, while the consequences for unacceptable behaviour were clearly outlined. The sportsmaster took Buddy under his wing, and Buddy underwent some counselling.

Buddy was not suspended again.

Detentions and lines

A parent says ...

My son Greg is basically a good kid at home, but he's forever on detention at school, mainly for talking in class. In fact, if Greg hasn't been on detention for a week, I crack open the champagne. Can't the school find some other way to punish him instead of depriving him of play, or can't they get him to enjoy school a bit more?

Before we become too defensive, it is wise to recognise the limited powers that a school has, and to remember that, where possible, it really is a good idea to support the school. Detentions can be useful for kids who rough-house in the playground or who need some cooling-off time.

The first thing to do is to contact the teacher and find out why your child has been put on detention (or 'arvos', as some kids call after-school detention). It may be worth calling the school counsellor, too, to find out what they recommend you do about the child's behaviour.

If your child behaves well at home and only plays up at school, there is a fair possibility that he is covering up either a learning problem or a social rejection problem, and is salvaging a badly bruised ego by clowning around. Check with the teacher and try to work out a plan of action by which any improvements are praised and which uses different penalties that actually teach the child something to remedy the problem. This may mean having lunch at different times to the other kids, doing chores, checking in with the principal each lunchtime or, a favourite: practising good habits every lunch session until they're sure they've got the message. Some schools use detention to chat to kids about different ways to deal with a situation.

But let us affirm our loathing for 'line-writing' detention. It achieves nothing useful: the kids don't feel any remorse, and all that happens is that their hand gets tired and they grow to hate writing.

Excursions and trips away

Ask any adult – the best memories he or she will have of school are playtimes, excursions and fun times.

With the happy memories comes the pain. There are few incursions on family sanity that match the school excursion: 'Where's the note? I can't go if I don't have the note!', 'Have you signed it yet, Mum?', 'How can I go wearing all this stupid stuff?', 'I won't need a jumper, none of the other kids are taking one!', 'Just drop me and go, don't wait around for the bus, it's so embarrassing when parents do that!'

Then, of course, the shy or sensitive or bed-wetting kids have their own crises of confidence to beat. The reality is that excursions and camps do a lot to bond a group of kids together, to develop confidence, and to give an insight into a different lifestyle to those who live daily in the normal rush and bustle of home life.

Most schools have fairly clear and strict rules about excursion behaviour and dress, so don't get conned about not having to wear a uniform, or that no notification about the excursion was given – the notification has probably been securely 'stored' in the bottom of your child's schoolbag for weeks. Many kids who have dressed to look 'cool' are left at the school gate, sadly waving after the departing bus.

If there is a difficulty with the cost of an excursion, many schools have a special fund for needy families, available through the principal.

What to do

▶ Get a copy of the excursion note if your child has been forgetful; schools keep spare copies.

▶ Put return notes and money in an envelope with your child's name, class and teacher and, if your child is forgetful, put it in their lunchbox or pencil case. They're sure to look there sometime in the day.

▶ Check the requirements for the excursion, to get the maximum benefit.

▶ If it is an outdoor excursion, think about the need for sunblock and hats.

▶ Reinforce the benefit of excursion-based education.

▶ Ask the teacher to link a shy child up with a buddy, so he will not be quite so scared of it all.

A true tale ... Sinead

Sinead's class was going on an excursion to the snow, but the cost was $350. Unsurprisingly, that amount was daunting for her parents in one lump sum. But the excursion was an opportunity for some real fun, friendship and fibre-building – particularly as Sinead had recently become a little withdrawn and manipulative. Her father set the ball rolling by suggesting he was willing to pay half. They sat down to work out ways she could earn the rest, beginning with a weekly chore chart. They figured that this would raise half the necessary sum. As well, Sinead and her friends set up a carwash to make a bit more. Before long, Sinead not only had the money, but a new ski jacket and a new brand of self-confidence too.

School camps

School camps are a special breed of excursion, and have the potential to be one of the most thrilling – and the most terrifying – experiences in a school kid's life. If parents and children are confident personalities, then camp is terrific; but if either the kids or their parents lack confidence, school camps can be a frightening spectre, because kids sense the anxiety and the fear of separation, and feel very insecure about the unknown.

For many insecure kids, school camp has been a real stepping-stone to growing up. Many sad, departing faces come back as smiling, stronger faces. If your child is really petrified, a few simple precautions will ease the pain:

❖ Make sure that your child has had some practice in sleeping away from home and, better still, sleeping out of doors.

❖ If your child is likely to baulk at going at the last minute, arrange for him to be picked up by a friend's family on the morning – this can prevent about 60 percent of 'barrier refusals'. At the assembly point, make sure they team up with a friend: friends are the big fear-beaters.

❖ Be positive. It is more than likely that a much more positive child will be returned to you.

❖ See if the teacher has a bright brochure – a few glossy pictures are better than imagined terrors.

❖ Try not to overreact either way if your kids say they don't want to go. They will feel different, isolated and inferior if everyone else is talking about the experience and they have been left out. Listen, share your similar childhood anxieties, and try to find out where the resistance is coming from:

 – If it is from loneliness, they should be 'buddied up' with a friend or two before the camp.

 – If it's because your child is a bed-wetter, have a chat to your doctor – there are medications and nasal sprays that can temporarily halt bed-wetting. But, strangely enough, just being away from home and sleeping in a different bed can often produce dry nights, perhaps because the child doesn't sleep quite as soundly.

- If it's just fear of the unknown, invite other kids over who have already been to camp (preferably at the same place) and really loved it.
- If it's because they'll miss Mum, let them take a little security keepsake, or write out what you will be doing while they're away, or get permission for a phone call if they want contact. You can even give them a map and draw a line from home – it never seems quite so far on paper, especially if it's a map of Australia or the whole world!

But the best advice is to alert the camp leader about your child's worries so that special duties or company can be found if spirits start to sag.

A true tale ... Andrew

Andrew was great at sports, well liked and very polite. But he felt really homesick whenever he was away from his mum. Mum came to see us before a camp to let us know he would have trouble. We worked out a little plan – plenty of practice over the holidays: sleeping at Nan's and at friends' to help build up his (and Mum's) confidence. We let the teacher know, so Andrew could be buddied up or put into a hut with kids he liked. And then we let Mum know that he could phone her, and to be prepared to pick him up if necessary. The first year, we got Andrew onto the bus after tears and, in so doing, broke down one of the hurdles. At camp during the day he was fine, but at night he had to phone Mum, who came and collected him. There was no shame and definitely no blame – Andrew was just learning his own lessons.

The next year, we got Andrew to sleep. Yes, there were tears after dinner but some kind words from a caring teacher and peer support moved him on to taking on the challenge – one night at a time. And during the day, the activities were too good to miss.

Home schooling

For some parents, home schooling has become a real alternative to public or private school. There are many different reasons why parents choose to home-school: dissatisfaction with the progress of their children, behaviour problems at school, concerns about the bad behaviour or bad influence of peers at school, religious convictions, an educational vision for their children, concern about the whole child, not just the pupil, etc. While some home educators follow a correspondence course, others work from textbooks. Some follow State education department curricula, others passionately believe in 'natural' learning – with the education building upon the children's own interests.

This form of education is becoming more popular. But before disgruntled, disillusioned or disappointed parents head down this road, there are several key considerations:

❖ It is not cheaper.

❖ It takes an enormous commitment from parents to sustain the effort over the long term.

❖ It does jeopardise children's social development and ability to get on with peers, unless home educators take steps to ensure that social opportunities are supplemented.

❖ It means that parents and children don't get much of a break from each other – that may not be an issue in the short term but it can wear thin if parents find their kids stressful.

❖ It means that parents must keep pace with curriculum expectations if they don't want their child to be at a disadvantage if and when formal schooling is resumed.

❖ Unless the parent knows how to teach and manage behaviour easily and adequately, there will be problems in disciplining the kids.

❖ There is a danger that 'education' can take over the whole house and the whole family. Children will resent being permanent pupils.

❖ The daily commitment of time to the kids is a real consideration – not just to teach, but also to do all the other childcare duties, and then prepare material for the next classes.

- ❖ Although not all home educators are registered (and there's a strong case why they should be), those who are, are inspected regularly by the State education authority. Some parents may not welcome such intrusion.
- ❖ There is also the need to find time to in-service and self-educate, so that the children are not disadvantaged vis-a-vis their school mates.
- ❖ Some parents may resent the lack of private space and time away from the children.

There are home-schooling support groups in most communities now, and education authorities can inform parents of those contacts (as can the Internet). But it's not a form of education for the faint-hearted or for those lacking real commitment to its principles. Parents contemplating such a move are strongly advised to discuss it at length within the family, with educators they respect, and to visit several other home educators to get some inside information.

A true tale ... Alicia

Alicia was different, and she knew it. The other kids always chose her last for any group activity, and she would come home crying: 'They whisper and laugh at me when I go to play with them, then they run away'. Mum was cranky with the school for not fixing the problem, and wanted to home-school Alicia. I felt strongly that that would just make her feel even more different and less capable of making friends, so we found a 'friends' group' (comprising other lonely kids) to develop her social skills. The class teacher also did a long project on 'differences' and respect. We also got Alicia involved in a horse-riding group, which she loved. But Mum felt things were not happening fast enough, so she withdrew her to home-school her.

Since then, Alicia has made a lot of friends who are also being home-schooled. But, at last check, she does not enjoy having her mum as her teacher, and Mum feels very unappreciated for all the time and career sacrifices she has made.

Appendix I: Learning with 'special needs'

'Special needs' are individual needs. It is easy to feel upset, defensive and protective if you find your child being labelled as having special needs – especially when she is young. Labels can be very emotive – especially those that describe disorders or disabilities. But if we consider special needs to be individual needs, we will be more understanding of the great diversity that shapes us as people, and as learners. Creativity and inventiveness stem from our unique qualities.

The reality is that children with specific learning differences do have to work harder to overcome weaknesses. These kids really benefit from strategies that can help them to level the playing field.

As outlined in Part Two, the greatest predictor of adult success for children with learning difficulties (and, we believe, all children) is a positive outlook. This requires parents to promote independence while retaining their love and support. Research that followed 41 men and women for over 20 years confirms that a positive attitude (i.e. accepting personal learning difficulties while focusing on what we do well) is the key to future success and happiness as adults – more so than IQ scores and good grades at school!

As parents, you need to have open communication channels and remain interested, but there comes a time when you have to let go and step back. It is hard to let go when it goes against our urge to care, but being a control freak and overprotective has negative side effects, even though we may have the best intentions at heart.

How to handle a 'label' given to your child

❖ Don't overreact – labels are often necessary to get assistance and funding.
❖ Without your positive outlook, your child may condemn herself as a lesser person.

❖ Keep in mind that we are all different; a difference may become a disability in certain environments (e.g. school) but not in others.

❖ Be prepared to research the label or disability, so you can become a caring and assertive advocate for your child's needs. No-one should know your child better than you.

As researcher and author Priscilla Vail comments:

> 'Labels are dangerous when they replace a person's humanity and individuality, but they are invaluable when they provide the precise terminology to decide who needs what, when, where, why, and how.'

ADD/ADHD

Let us state from the outset that ADD/ADHD is a real condition, although it is often over-diagnosed by hurried doctors and stressed parents and/or teachers. The actual neurological basis of ADD/ADHD remains unidentified, but there is a strong suggestion of immaturity in the pre-frontal cortex (frontal lobe), which is the executive lobe of the brain and helps with organising, inhibiting, sequencing, planning and other such measures of self-control. There is also evidence that the right parietal lobe may be implicated – this is a part of the brain that assists children in coping with stress. If this exploratory research identifies a common phenomenon in ADD/ADHD sufferers, then it would help explain why these children don't cope well when there is excessive stress, over-stimulation or over-complexity in their environment. ADD/ADHD is diagnosed by using checklists from parents and teachers to see how a child's behaviour is relative to a norm. The symptoms are on a spectrum, ranging from mild to severe.

ADD/ADHD affects concentration and focus. There is increasing evidence that ADD/ADHD is an inherited condition: identical twins have 75–91 percent chance of sharing the condition, and children with ADD/ADHD are likely to have a close relative who also has ADD/ADHD.

The US National Institutes of Health estimates that between 3 and 5 percent of children have ADD/ADHD, which means that in a classroom of 25–30 children, it is likely that at least one will have ADD/ADHD.

There are three 'clusters' within ADD/ADHD:

1 inattention: poor listening, concentration
2 impulsivity: acts before thinking, does dangerous/risky things, and
3 hyperactivity: always on the go, restless.

Just because a child may not be hyperactive does not mean that she doesn't struggle with inattention or impulsivity.

Children with ADD/ADHD may frequently switch from one thing to another at the drop of a hat. They have impulses, and they act on them. They can be exhausting for parents. ADD/ADHD is diagnosed using behaviour checklists filled in by parents and teachers, and by a thorough assessment with a child psychologist.

Treatment

The appropriate treatment of ADD/ADHD is a very controversial topic, with professional opinions ranging from strongly pro-medication to vehemently anti-medication, with the middle ground favouring some medication (for at least a 12-month period) in conjunction with individual behavioural and educational assistance. There is a number of new techniques for treating and monitoring ADD/ADHD that involve brain scanning, cerebellum stimulation, the administration of Omega 3 or 6, and other approaches. If you are concerned that your child may have ADD/ADHD, consult an expert and investigate the latest research, as new schools of thought emerge with some regularity. A couple of excellent books for families dealing with ADD/ADHD are by Dr Geoff Kewley and Dr Brenton Prosser, respectively (see 'Resources').

Behavioural techniques

Behavioural techniques (often used in conjunction with medication) have proved very effective in treating ADD/ADHD. Parents wanting to pursue this treatment are advised to consult Dr John's *A Handbook for Happy Families* or the accompanying *Happy Families* DVD series, especially the six–eleven years DVD or the *Reparations* DVD.

Skills training can also be beneficial. As the problem appears to lie in the brain's neurotransmitters, thereby leaving the child vulnerable to 'scatty' behaviour, considerable benefit can be gained by practising the desired behaviour till it becomes dominant in the child's behaviour repertoire.

Nutrition: Omega 3 oils

In 2005, Durham County Council in the UK held a trial involving two groups of children given supplements during school: one was given Omega 3 and Omega 6 evening primrose oil, the other was given a placebo of olive oil. The BBC reported the 'results suggested that after three months, the group using the Omega oils made "highly significant improvements" on 12 out of 13 behavioural scales, including the three diagnostic ADHD features – inattention, hyperactivity and impulsivity. Short-term memory also significantly improved'. However, there have been too few rigorous studies to verify the Omega 3 effectiveness at this point to comment further.

Other strategies

❖ Schedule and use a calendar – establish routines for the day, from waking up to bedtime. Structure times and make them visible on a planner.

❖ Organise and place items – have a specific place for specific things, and establish a routine, e.g. when your child comes home, ensure the school bag goes in the right place – not just dumped at the door.

❖ Use organising aids – training your child to jot down things that need to be remembered is important. Encourage your child to create lists, and to use coloured folders for specific topics – such as a red folder for homework to do, a blue folder for homework completed.

Receptive language disorder (RLD)

RLD causes a child to struggle to understand spoken and sometimes written language. Children with RLD have trouble communicating with others, expressing themselves and organising their thoughts. RLD children struggle to find the connection between words and their meanings.

Strategies

Consult a speech therapist, who may advise on a program which focuses on the link between sounds, letters and words. Consider building word lists, and role-play for vocabulary used in social settings.

Dyslexia

Dyslexia is probably the best-known specific learning difficulty, but there is also a lot of misinformation associated with it. Letter-reversing is commonly held up as an indication of dyslexia – but this can be a normal developmental stage as children learn to master letter formations. A current scientific hypothesis is that dyslexia is an immaturity in phonological awareness – the ability to match sounds to letters. This makes it difficult to analyse the sounds of words, which impacts on spelling. This theory seems to be supported by brain scans that highlight a deficit in connections between auditory and visual processing.

Dyslexia is a neurobiological condition that affects about 10 percent of people. It does not affect a person's intelligence. It is life-long, so children with dyslexia need to strengthen strategies to best support their individual learning needs.

Strategies

As dyslexia is a broad term, with a spectrum of behaviours and conditions associated with it, not all strategies work for all people. No intervention should be attempted without the professional advice of a remedial reading teacher and/or an educational psychologist.

❖ Link up with SPELD or whichever support group is in your area for children with a reading disability.
❖ Use a mind map to outline big-picture thoughts – don't focus on spelling or punctuation at the drafting stage of a writing exercise.
❖ Consider visually illustrating each thought or idea rather than using words.
❖ Tape-record ideas for playback later.
❖ Encourage your child to read aloud as she writes.
❖ Foster good keyboard skills.
❖ 'Chunk' ideas into smaller activities or tasks.
❖ Use different-coloured highlighters and folders to organise the material and the key points.
❖ Promote the writing process – Plan, Draft, Edit, Publish.

❖ Prioritise tasks and schedule time, thereby establishing good routines.

❖ Use software programs that support learning.

Software to assist reading and writing

❖ *Voice-recognition software* converts a child's spoken language into text – not always with the best results, unless you like synthetic accents! This area is set to develop further over the coming years and offers great opportunity for the support of specific learning difficulties.

❖ *Read and Write Gold* – this program reads text. Worksheets can be scanned, and then the program will read that text aloud.

❖ *Mind-map software,* such as Inspiration or other free programs, offer great visual planning systems.

❖ *ThinkMap Visual Thesaurus* – this is an online program that maps out words and associated links visually.

❖ *Clicker5* – a fantastic program that gives information on topics in full multimedia.

❖ *TextEase* – a program that will allow children to hear words they write.

Dyspraxia

Children with dyspraxia can understand instructions but they struggle to demonstrate or state what they have learned. Dyspraxia is a condition that makes motor skills, such as coordination, speech, balance and movement, difficult for children. It is a neurological disorder that results in messages not being transmitted properly: children know what they want to do or say, but get frustrated because their body or their mouth muscles won't do it. It is 70 percent more likely to occur in boys than girls, and it seems that there is one child in every 30 who has the condition. There can be different effects and implications, as with all learning needs. Children with dyspraxia are often disorganised, can find communication a struggle, and can experience social issues, because they can seem immature.

Poor handwriting is one of the most common symptoms, but there are many other characteristics that need to be considered. There are three different classes of dyspraxia:

1 *verbal* – the processing and making of speech
2 *oral* – sounds and movements of the mouth not associated with speech, e.g. licking, sucking, salivating, and
3 *motor* – the coordination and balance associated with movement (fine and gross motor control).

Strategies

Consult a speech therapist for verbal or oral dyspraxia, or an occupational therapist if it's a motor problem. You may be advised to break complex tasks down into step-by-step directions. You may also be advised to build up to more complex activities, encouraging easy physical activities that develop coordination. Offering tasks that allow success will build confidence as each area is mastered.

Dyscalculia

Dyscalculia is to Mathematics what dyslexia is to reading. Dyscalculia is a broad term used to describe a specific learning disability in Mathematics. It is estimated that 4 percent of students reveal symptoms of dyscalculia. They may be talented in other subject areas, but just don't seem to 'get' Maths – counting or the processes involved in calculating answers. This learning difficulty can lead to frustration and anxiety with Maths.

Strategies

Dyscalculia is not as widely known as dyslexia. Consult your child's teacher, and refer to the section on Mathematics in Part Three of this book.

Obsessive-compulsive disorder (OCD)

Upsetting intrusive thoughts and/or repetitive actions that interfere with the individual's daily functioning characterise this disorder. It becomes noticeable in kids aged between 10 and 24, and it is just as common in girls as in boys. With this disorder, the individual expresses either obsessions or compulsions.

Obsessions are defined by the following four criteria:

1 Recurrent and persistent thoughts, impulses or images are experienced at some time during the disturbance as intrusive and inappropriate, and cause marked anxiety and distress.

2 The thoughts, impulses or images are not simply worries about real-life problems.

3 The person attempts to suppress or ignore such thoughts, impulses or images, or to neutralise them with some other thought or action.

4 The person recognises that the obsessive thoughts, impulses or images are a product of her own mind (and not imposed from without).

Compulsions are defined by the following two criteria:

1 The person feels driven to perform a 'ritual' of repetitive behaviours (e.g. hand-washing, ordering, checking) or mental acts (e.g. counting, repeating words silently).

2 The behaviours are structured to prevent or reduce distress, or to prevent some dreaded event or situation from happening, but without a logical reason.

Strategies

Be aware of your child's fears, and their different levels: some things cause more distress than others. Map out explicitly the obsessions and/or compulsions, and their triggers.

Be supportive, and maintain the focus on the OCD – not the child – as the problem. Children with OCD know that it doesn't make sense, so don't reprimand them by saying things like, 'That's crazy! Stop it! Control yourself!'

Get your child to picture the OCD as a thing or a character, and then coach the child to speak her mind back to the OCD aloud, e.g. 'Pull your head in, OCD!' or 'Get back in your box – I didn't let you out!' Use this strategy only on the specific things you are trying to remedy, and don't try to tackle too many at once. Also, don't actually name the fear (e.g. 'I won't get hurt if I don't count all the steps') while using this strategy – that just cements the worry, and can promote a compulsion.

Celebrate any success as if you are a team making giant leaps of success: rewards empower the child to see the control she has over OCD.

Parents are advised to seek professional consultation with a paediatrician and a clinical child psychologist if they have any concerns in this area.

Autism spectrum disorders (ASD)

Autism is a disorder that appears in early childhood. It is usually associated with poor social skills and an inability to understand language and nonverbal cues, especially emotional expressions. The usual indicators are repetitive and strange behaviours, which the child feels compelled to do. If a routine is disrupted, the child can become very distressed. This may sound like many children in their early years, and here lies the issue: like all disorders, there is a spectrum of behaviours and tendencies. Autism has a wide range of characteristics, from mild to disabling.

Dr Simon Baren-Cohen suggests that autism leads to 'mindblindness' – where autistic children lack awareness that other people have their own thoughts, plans and points of view. This is one hypothesis for why autistic children seem socially inept and lack empathy. Research suggests a neurological cause related to the atypical function and structure of the amygdala area of the brain.

There are usually two stages to diagnosis. The first is screening, using behaviour checklists and observations that teachers and parents will be expected to complete, rating observed behaviour on a scale based on a norm. The second stage requires a comprehensive diagnostic evaluation by professionals, particularly a clinical child psychologist.

Asperger syndrome (AS)

Asperger syndrome is specific on the spectrum of behaviours associated with autism. The *DSM-IV* states that: 'The essential features of Aspergers Disorder are severe and sustained impairment in social interaction ... and the development of restricted, repetitive patterns of behaviour, interests, and activities ...'.

A distinction between Asperger syndrome and autism is that children with Asperger usually have somewhat normal language development.

Strategies

If you would like to find out if your child has Asperger syndrome, or if you would like some assistance with management strategies, you could consult the excellent book by Dr Tony Attwood (see 'Resources'). You may also like to consult a clinical psychologist – preferably one who specialises in Asperger management – for support and strategies.

Pervasive developmental disorders (PDD)

This term causes distress among parents whose child is so diagnosed. It is being replaced with the more appropriate Autism spectrum disorders (ASD). This diagnosis just means that a child has behaviour attributable to a range of autistic tendencies but does not meet the selection criteria to be diagnosed accurately into one area.

Semantic-pragmatic disorder (SPD)

Initially defined in 1983, Semantic-pragmatic Disorder refers to learners who take conversations and details very literally, which means they struggle with the meaning and social context of conversational topics. These children are on the autism spectrum. They don't seem to understand nuances of language, and find it difficult to comprehend or discuss a central issue. A child with SPD tends to focus on the literal details of a conversation, which results in the child interpreting and re-telling it just as it was heard. This can lead to social problems in group situations, or butting in while others are talking. It often presents itself as a bitter playground conflict whereby other kids 'cheat' or 'don't play fair' – i.e. they don't see things the way the child with SPD sees them.

However, in a one-to-one or a home environment, interaction can seem very normal. In brief, children with SPD have a problem with listening and with processing the meaning of language.

Strategies

If your child says something incorrect, repeat the same phrase correctly to reinforce how it should be said. Use pictures, colours, sounds and actions when introducing a new word or concept. And don't tackle too much too soon: let your child consolidate her understanding of each key word, term or phrase.

Give instructions that are very literal in expectations – don't use sarcasm, metaphors or puns. Show everyday situations and have discussions about them, with the child discussing them in her own words. SPD children can mimic adult language and intonation very well – which sometimes makes them seem very mature. However, they do not fully understand things and, when asked to recount what has happened, they struggle to explain a situation or an event.

It may be useful to enrol your child in a drama or a social-skills program. And restrict any viewing of violent TV shows, DVDs or video games.

Remember that your child may need ongoing help to distinguish what is real from what is not.

Conduct disorder (CD)

Conduct disorder is a serious disruptive behavioural problem that may involve the repetitive violation of a person or animal, their rights or their property. Violations are usually aggressive, and fall into one of the following categories:

- ❖ aggression to people and animals
- ❖ destruction of property
- ❖ deceitfulness or theft, or
- ❖ serious violation of rules.

Conduct disorder is typically diagnosed betweem the ages of 10 and 16, and usually impacts heavily on families. This is a serious disorder that requires immediate professional psychiatric intervention. Children with CD are at increased risk of mental illness, drug abuse and personality disorders as adults. Parenting style and family factors do increase the risk factor.

Strategies

Strategies for treating CD include behaviour therapy, parent management training and functional family therapy.

Oppositional defiant disorder (ODD)

All children can be defiant at times, and with good reason if they're tired, hungry or feeling sick. However, if there is consistent negative, hostile and defiant behaviour, with at least four of the following criteria present, you need to consult a professional.

- ❖ Frequently loses their temper.
- ❖ Often argues with adults.
- ❖ Actively defies or refuses to comply with adults' requests or rules.
- ❖ Tries to deliberately annoy people.
- ❖ Consistently blames others for her mistakes or misbehaviour (this can be common in teenagers!).
- ❖ Becomes touchy or easily annoyed by others.
- ❖ Is regularly angry and resentful.
- ❖ Is often spiteful or vindictive, seeking revenge.

The statistics suggest that 5–15 percent of children have ODD. It could be that there is another specific learning difficulty (such as ADHD) or a mood disorder (such as depression or anxiety) associated with the behaviour.

Strategies

- ❖ Look for positives, and praise the successes more than you reprimand the negative behaviour.
- ❖ Start your responses with a positive option, e.g. 'We will be having your favourite meal, if we can get ready for dinner early'.
- ❖ Use time-out strategies, and keep a calm but confident voice when showing authority.
- ❖ Take time out yourself – you need a break – and share the load with a partner or someone who can be a support.
- ❖ Use and stick to consequences that can be enforced – don't budge once you stake a claim on expectations.
- ❖ Check that your parental style is not confrontational or oppositional (remember that children copy their role-models!).

❖ Use Dr John's 'Reparations' model (in his DVD of the same title) to reduce conflict and build empathy in children with ODD.

❖ Consult a child psychologist for assessment and strategies.

Anaphylaxis and hyper-allergic conditions

Anaphylaxis isn't a specific learning difficulty, but it is worth mentioning it in this section because hyper-allergic conditions do affect learning. Children feel distracted and uncertain. It is also important we understand that diet plays a key role in learning.

Anaphylaxis is a serious allergic reaction, so serious it can become fatal, and the incidence is rapidly increasing. Some children are extremely sensitive to certain food products – peanuts are the most publicised cause of anaphylaxis. However, other common causes include other foods, medication, insect stings and latex.

These days, schools should be well equipped to manage anaphylactic reactions in children. If you know your child is anaphylactic, the use of an Epi-pen (which gives a quick shot of adrenaline) is vital.

Appendix II: The wiring of thinking

The basic element of learning resides in the wiring of the brain. From the moment we are born, we start losing brain cells. Children have more possible connections than us 'oldies'. They dream of dinosaurs, draw amazing scenes, explore strange imaginary worlds, and role-model wonderful games with dolls, building blocks and old cardboard cartons. They are creative.

Imagine that the network of possible connections in the brain is like a wheat field. If we walk through a wheat field for the very first time, and look behind us, we see only the wheat – there is no path, we have to make our own. However, if we walk through that wheat field again and again and again, following the same path, we will soon see a clear track. And when we have a clear track, we will follow it, preferring to walk along that path rather than trample more wheat. It becomes easier. And because it becomes easier, we use it more often.

This is how habits are formed – and why we must model behaviours, set expectations (so pathways are created) and establish good routines (so movement on the pathways is repeated).

The neuron – the basic element of the brain's wiring

Knowing how we learn is all about knowing how our brain functions. The VAK model (see pages 68–69) highlights the organic nature of learning. It represents learning as much more than just knowing content. Learning relies on engagement for the development of deeper understanding. This means the learner has to concentrate to form connections, linking something new with something known. These connections, or pathways, are buried deep in our brain's wiring for thinking, and involve cells called neurons. Like a good mechanic, it is important we have a solid grasp of how the 'motor' works under our bonnet. The neurons are the wiring.

The neuron is a little like an arm with extended fingers. The extended fingers are called dendrites. Each dendrite is linked to thousands of other neurons by proximity. The dendrites feed into the soma, a roundish area like your palm that contains the battery or power plant, called the nucleus. Where we have a wrist, the neuron has a hump. If a signal is strong enough, it will pass over the hump and travel down the axon, which is just like our arm. The axon stretches away, carrying signals to other 'terminal buttons'. Around the axon is a protective coating, called the myelin sheath. It is like the sleeve of a coat: the thicker the myelin sheath coating, the more protection it gives the transmission down the axon, which makes the signal stronger. This signal then hits the terminal button and passes across a gap – like getting off a train at a station – to another neuron. This synaptic gap is how messages are transferred. There are 1000–10,000 synapses for a 'typical' neuron. Just like at a station, the closer we are to the platform, the better the message transfers. To help with this transfer, there are chemicals in the brain that form a bridge across from the terminal button of one cell to another neuron – these are called neurotransmitters.

Two major areas for learning, where our brain makes connections, are the movement of signals down the axon, and the transmission across the synaptic gap. These areas impact on concentration, forming connections, and staying on task.

The 'triune brain' theory

The human brain has not had an upgrade for over 100,000 years. One theory about its recent evolution is that it has developed in three stages. This is called the 'triune brain' theory. These three stages are:

1 *The reptilian complex* – this is the primitive part of the brain. It consists of the brain stem and the cerebellum. Its purpose is for physical survival by automatic responses. It deals with all the subconscious acts – breathing, blinking, digestion, etc. It is the part of the brain that executes the 'fight, freeze or flight' response.

2 *The limbic system* – this is the area that involves emotion. It includes two little groups of cells, called the amygdala, which associate events with emotion. This theory suggests that the limbic system overrides the reptilian complex because our memory (based on emotions) emphasises how we respond.

3 *The neocortex* – this is the final evolutionary stage of our brain's development. The neocortex is the outer portion of the brain and accounts for about five-sixths of its size. This is the area that makes language, and where we process information to make rational decisions.

All three areas interact via an extensive network of nerves. The processing of information is relayed back and forth, to and from the limbic system and the neocortex. This feedback loop is the interplay of emotion and memory, thought and action.

Why we overreact – 'the amygdala hijack'

We've all been in a situation where we have 'lost it'. You are driving along, and another driver behaves in a way that makes you angry – you react emotionally. Later, you think to yourself, 'Hmmm, that was weird – why did I do that?' You were 'hijacked' – or rather, your actions and thoughts were. This is how it happens:

1 A stimulus comes in to our limbic system processor, the amygdala.

2 The amygdala filters the stimulus and passes on the information in one of two ways:

　i) If the stimulus is stressful or a threat, the amygdala will pass the message to the reptilian brain. We will subconsciously react: fight, flight or freeze. Our kids might throw down their pen, hurl their book, and yell!

　ii) The information is passed on to the neocortex, where we can associate the thought with language, and consider our responses. This is where we become rational. Grandma's advice makes a lot of sense: take three deep breaths and count to ten. In doing this, we process our response.

Kids function just like adults, but without the many strategies that adults (hopefully) have acquired to overcome emotional outbursts and poorly-considered reactions. To get children to take control, we must switch on their awareness of what their primitive brain is doing. We must develop in our children self-coping strategies so they can become independent thinkers. We need to switch them on so they thrive at school – in the classroom and, most importantly, as learners!

Authors' notes

Page 6 'Researcher Georgia Kamperos has found that "boys and girls achieved better results when they attended single-sex schools".': Kamperos, G. (2000) *Academic Achievements of Girls & Boys*, In Alliance, Sydney University.

Page 6 '... research finds that girls are much more active in play when they are not competing with boys for play space.': Archer, J. 'Childhood Gender Roles: Social Context and Organisation', in McGurk, H. (ed) (1992), *Childhood Social Development: Contemporary Perspectives*, Psychology Press, UK.

Page 8 '... there has been an increase of about 18,000 students (1.6 percent) per year in private school enrolments, compared to a 0.1 percent increase for public schools.': *Australian Bureau of Statistics*, (2006) Schools Australia, 4221.0.

Page 9 '... there's also other research which suggests that at university level public school students are better survivors ...': Dobson, I. 2005, 'State school students 'do better at uni', http://www.abc.net.au/news/newsitems/200504/s1339356.htm, accessed December 2007.

Page 14 '... children are at greatest risk at times of greatest change.': Bronfenbrenner, U., (1975). *Influences on Human Development*, Holt.

Page 20 'Research shows clearly that kids do better at school if their parents are involved in some way.': 'Getting Involved in Your Child's Education', http://www.nea.org/parents/index.html accessed December 2007.

Page 34 'the basic need for survival plus the four psychological needs of belonging, power, freedom and fun': Glasser, W. (1992). *Choice Theory: A New Psychology of Personal Freedom*, Harper Collins.

Page 37 'This can lead to what psychologists term "learned helplessness".': Seligman, M.E.P. (1990) *Learned Optimism*, Knopf, New York.

Page 42 '... "habits of the mind".': Costa, A.L., Kallick, B. (2000). *Habits of Mind: A Developmental Series (books 1–4)*, Hawker Brownlow, Melbourne.

Page 48 'Dr Jamie McKenzie worries that children today have electronic shovels that cut and paste other people's ideas ...': McKenzie, J. (2005) *Learning to Question to Wonder to Learn*, FNO Press, Bellingham, US.

Page 52 'Professor Howard Gardiner suggests that there are many types of intelligence ...': Gardiner, H. (1983) *Frames of Mind: The Theory of Multiple Intelligences*, Basic Books.

Page 52 'There is also another aspect of intelligence ...': Matthews, G., Zeidner, M. and Roberts, R.D. (2002) *Emotional Intelligence: Science and Myth*. MIT Press, Cambridge, US.

Page 52 'Furthermore, Thomas Friedman ... highlights, via the equation CQ + PQ > IQ, that curiosity (CQ) and passion (PQ) are far more important than intelligence (IQ) for successful learning': ' Friedman, T.L. (2005), *The World is Flat: A Brief History of the 21st Century.* Farrar, Straus and Giroux, New York.

Page 80 **'We have used the Dolch list of sight words ...'**: http://gemini.es.brevard.k12.fl.us/sheppard/reading/dolch.html accessed on 10 July, 2007.

Page 93 **'... research has highlighted the importance of stressing letter sounds in words.'**: Wesley A. Hoover, 'The Importance of Phonemic Awareness in Learning to Read', http://www.sedl.org/pubs/sedl-letter/v14n03/3.html, accessed December 2007.

Page 94 **'One long-time favourite book is *Teach Your Child to Spell* ...'**: Cheetham, J. (1993) *Teach Your Child to Spell: A Simple Solution to Improve Spelling and Build Your Child's Confidence,* Hyland House.

Page 99 **'A Mathematical Dictionary for Schools'**: Bolt, B., Hobbs, D. (1998) *A Mathematical Dictionary for Schools,* Cambridge UP.

Page 111 **'Research shows that the best way to deal with bullying is to get bystanders to stand up and do what is right.'**: Lodge, J., Frydenberg, E., 'The Role of Peer Bystanders in School Bullying: Positive Steps Toward Promoting Peaceful Schools' in *Theory Into Practice,* v44 n4, 2005, pp.329–336. Lawrence Erlbaum Associates, Mahwah, NJ.

Page 112 **'Being a bully increases by six times the chance of having a criminal conviction by the age of eighteen.'**: Australian Broadcasting Commission, http://www.abc.net.au/news/stories/2007/07/11/1975619.htm?section=justin; accessed on 11 July 2007.

Page 112 **'And research from Norway suggests that parents of bullies show some common traits ...'**: Olweus, D. (1999) in P.K. Smith, Y. Morita, J. Junger-Tas, D. Olweus, R. Catalano, and P. Slee (eds), *The Nature of School Bullying: A cross-national perspective* (pp.7–27), Routledge, London.

Page 120 **'... an "Online Safety for Teens" survey reveals ...'**: Conducted by NetAlert and Nine MSN. See NetAlert: http://www.netalert.net.au accessed on 29 July 2007.

Page 128 **'... dieticians tell us that 60 percent of deaths are diet-related!'**: Lindenmayer, I. (2002) 'Food Labels: A Matter of Life and Death' http://www.foodstandards.gov.au/newsroom/speeches/speeches2002/speechianlindenmayer1757.cfm accessed on 28 July 2007.

Page 130 **'That's the only conclusion to be reached after reading Sue Dengate's book *Fed Up* ...'**: Dengate, S. (1998). *Fed Up,* Random House, Sydney.

Page 130 **'Dengate claims that children who are irritable, restless, inattentive, moody ...'**: Dengate goes further: in one study she quotes of 140 people with behavioural symptoms, 74 percent reacted to salicylates or the chemicals in some fruits, 67 percent reacted to preservatives, 54 percent reacted to food colouring, 41 percent to antioxidants, 40 percent to amines, and 39 percent to MSG.

Page 130 **'... programs such as "Management Sense Food Sense" from Focis...'**: http://www.focis.com.au/resources.php, accessed on 26 July 2007.

Page 130 '**... evidence suggests that children perform better in the classroom if they have had a healthy start to the day ...**': 'The Role of Sound Nutrition and Physical Activity in Academic Achievement', http://www.actionforhealthykids.org/filelib/facts_and_findings/nutrition,%20physical%20activity%20and%20achievement.pdf, accessed December 2007.

Page 140 '**... some research has found that computer competence actually helps to enhance social skills.**': 'Using Computers to Develop Preschoolers' Social Skills, http://factsinaction.org/classroom/clmay03.htm, accessed December 2007.

Page 144 '**In a study, little kids drew family pictures with Dad in close, but nine- to twelve-year-olds drew Dad as more distant.**': As recalled by Dr John Irvine; source unidentified.

Page 144 '**... "If a father's not there, it's like driving on two cylinders instead of four"**, Edgar, D. (2005). *The War Over Work: The Future of Work and Family*, Melbourne UP.

Page 162 '**Ten commandments for parents' educational salvation**': Rimm, S., (1996) *Why Bright Kids Get Poor Grades: And What You Can Do About It*, Three Rivers Press, New York.

Page 184 '**... Research that followed 41 men and women for over 20 years confirms that a positive attitude ...**': 'Positive Attitude Trumps IQ, Good Grades as Success Predictor for LD Adults', http://www.schwablearning.org/articles.aspx?r=622; accessed on 20 May 2007.

Page 185 '**As researcher and author Priscilla Vail comments ...**': Vail, P. (2007). 'How to Detect Learning Problems in Your Child', http://www.schwablearning.org/articles.aspx?r=366; accessed on 20 May 2007.

Page 185 '**... There is also evidence ...**': Vance, A., 'New brain research from the University of Melbourne shows links to stress in ADHD children', http://uninews.unimelb.edu.au/articleid_4834.html, accessed December 2007.

Page 185 '**There is increasing evidence that ADD/ADHD is an inherited condition ...**': Lavelle, P., 'Fact File: ADHD', http://www.abc.net.au/health/library/stories/2003/04/24/1828304.htm, accessed December 2007.

Page 185 '**... between 3 and 5 percent of children have ADD/ADHD, which means that in a classroom of 25–30 children, it is likely that at least one will have ADD/ADHD**': National Institute of Mental Health (USA), http://www.nimh.nih.gov/publicat/adhd.cfm, accessed May 2007.

Page 187 '**The BBC reported the "results suggested that after three months, the group using the Omega oils made 'highly significant improvements' ..."**': British Broadcasting Corporation, http://news.bbc.co.uk/2/hi/uk_news/england/4511759.stm; accessed on 20 May 2007.

Page 189 '**A current scientific hypothesis is that dyslexia is an immaturity in phonological awareness – the ability to match sounds to letters.**': 'Dyslexia (Reading and Writing Problems)', http://www.autism-help.org/comorbid-dyslexia-autism.htm, accessed December 2007.

Page 190 '[Dyspraxia] ... is 70 percent more likely to occur in boys than girls, and it seems that there is one child in every 30 who has the condition.': 'What is Dyspraxia?', http://www.dyspraxia.com.au/, accessed December 2007.

Page 190 'It is estimated that 4 percent of students reveal symptoms of dyscalculia.': 'Root of dyscalculia found', http://www.news-medical.net/?id=22658, accessed December 2007.

Page 194 '... autism leads to "mindblindness"': Baron-Cohen, S. (1995). *Mindblindness: and essay on autism and theory of mind*, Boston, MIT Press/ Bradford Books.

Page 194 'Research suggests a neurological cause related to atypical function and structure of the amygdala area of the brain.': Baron-Cohen, S., Ring, H.A., Bullmore, E.T., Wheelwright, S., Ashwin, C., Williams, S.C.R.. 'The amygdala theory of autism', *Neuroscience and Biobehavioural Reviews*, 2000, 24, 355–364.

Page 194 'Asperger syndrome is specific on the spectrum of behaviours associated with autism. The *DSM-IV* states ...': American Psychiatric Association (2000), *Diagnostic and Statistical Manual of Mental Disorders IV – TR Fourth Edition*.

Page 196 'Strategies for treating CD include behaviour therapy, parent management training and functional family therapy...': The Australian Psychological Society, Better Health Channel: *Conduct Disorder*. http://www.betterhealth.vic.gov.au/ bhcv2/bhcarticles.nsf/pages/Conduct_disorder?OpenDocument/ accessed on 30 July 2007.

Page 197 'The statistics suggest that 5–15 percent of children have ODD.': American Psychiatric Association (2000), *Diagnostic and Statistical Manual of Mental Disorders IV – TR Fourth Edition*.

Page 200 'The human brain has not had an upgrade for over 100,000 years. One theory about its recent evolution ...': See Paul Maclean, *The Triune Brain in Evolution: Role in Paleocerebral Functions*, Springer, New York, 1990.

Acknowledgments

So many people have contributed to the tapestry of this book now, from the days when it was *Coping with School* to its revised form as *Thriving at School*, that a full roll-call would read like a passing parade of top educators. I'm hoping that their collective contribution will position this edition as the best possible book for parents trying to help their children at school. Rather than re-list all the contributors, I would refer readers back to earlier editions for details.

Some years ago, my brother Warwick and I – with the help of that great psychologist, Ian Wallace – hammered out the first edition of this book and I felt up to the mark. When it came to the second edition, I sought the help of some educational heavyweights – Dale Fotheringham, a school principal, and Bill Low, an Area Director of Education, along with numerous teachers – to add their specialist pieces. That got me through that edition, and it was received very well in the community.

So, without detracting from the wisdom of those who had helped so much before, I sought the assistance of one of the most dynamic and capable educators I have ever had the privilege of working beside. In my role as consultant psychologist to the Central Coast Grammar School, I came across this dynamic leader, John Stewart, Head of the Junior School, and I knew that between us we could produce a book that would make its mark. I hope readers find it as useful and sensible as we believe it to be.

When I wrote the last edition, I indicated that it would be the last, and I meant that. However, the encouragement of my wonderful publisher, Rex Finch, his editor, Sean Doyle, and the tireless energy and inspiration of my co-author, John Stewart, have allowed this entirely new, revised, updated and teacher/parent user-friendly version to be published. I thank them all, and I thank my wonderful family for giving me the belief that I still had so much to offer, and for encouraging me in this enterprise. And I thank John Stewart's family for their long suffering as he juggled this extensive revision in between running a school, shifting house, renovating the new house, painting, and finding time for his family.

Dr John Irvine

There are certain people who have been passengers on my voyage of discovery. They truly deserve mention.

I acknowledge the support of my wife, Sophie, and my family; David Moeller; my sister, Catherine – the greatest. I also thank Maree Gross and Roslyn Hayles – two of the best Kindergarten teachers you could hope to find; Heather Gill, Kate McGrath, Cathy Cross and Jacquie Payne for their willingness to read the rough draft and offer critical viewpoints, with positive comments. And I feel indebted to Sean Doyle for his thoroughness, patience and preparation, getting a draft into a very readable manuscript.

I was lucky to have the opportunity to work with Dr John, and thank him sincerely for his belief and total support. His wise and comforting words contained in this book celebrate the most important feature of our society: common sense.

John Stewart

Resources

If you would like to find more up-to-date information, share your thoughts with others, or find further resources, visit our website: http://thrivingatschool.com. The website follows the same structure as this book, with the content being divided into six corresponding sections.

Dr John's book *A Handbook for Happy Families* and the accompanying *Happy Families* DVD series, are available at http://www.drjohnirvine.com.

Suggested reading

Adams, C., Fay, J. & Loreen-Martin, J. *No is not Enough* Collins, London, 1984

Appleby, M. & King, R. *Be a Friend for Life: preventing youth suicide*, Rose Education, Narellan, 1992

Armstrong, T. *The Myth of the A.D.D. Child*, Penguin, NY, 1995

Attwood, T. *Asperger's Syndrome: A Guide for Parents and Professionals*. Jessica Kingsley Publishers, London, 1998

Bernard, M. & Hajzler, D. *You can do it*, Collins Dove, Sydney, 1987

Biddulph. S. *Raising Boys*, Finch Publishing, Sydney, 2003

Blankenhorn, D. *Fatherless in America*, Harper Collins, NY, 1995

Costa, A.L., Kallick, B. *Habits of Mind: A Developmental Series (books 1–4)*, Hawker Brownlow, Australia, 2000

Costa, A.L. (ed) *Developing Minds: A Resource Book for Teaching Thinking* (3rd ed), Association for Supervision and Curriculum Development, Virginia, USA, 2000

Covey. S. *Seven Habits of Highly Effective Families*, Allen & Unwin, Sydney, 1997

Darvey, W. & Powell, K. *What shall we tell the Children?* Hodder & Stoughton, Sydney, 1995

Darvey, W. & Powell, K. *The Puberty Book*, Hodder & Stoughton, Sydney, 1995

Dengate, S. *Fed Up: Understanding How Food Affects Your Child and What You Can Do About It*, Random House, Australia, 1998

Donaghy, B. *Leaving Early*, Harper Health, Sydney, 1997

Donaghy, B. *Unzipped*, Harper Collins, Sydney, 1997

Donahoo, D. *Idolising Children*, University of NSW, Australia, 2007

Dwyer, B. *Parents and Teachers as Partners*, PETA, Sydney, 1989

Ewing, R. (ed) *Beyond the Reading Wars: A balanced approach to helping children learn to read*, Primary English Teaching Association, 2006

Hills. A. & Stone, P. *Good Food for Kids*, Harper Collins, Sydney, 1995

Irvine, J.F. *A Handbook for Happy Families*, Finch Publishing, Sydney, 2002

Irvine, J.F. *Who'd be a Parent? The manual that should have come with the kids*, Pan Macmillan, Sydney, 1998

Kewley, G. *ADHD: Recognition, Reality and Resolution*, Australian Council for Educational Research, Melbourne, 2002

Kewley, G. *Attention Deficit Hyperactivity Disorder*, LAC Publications, London, 1998

Lever, R. *Guide to Childcare in Australia*, Penguin, Sydney, 1993

Lewis, G. *Bringing up your Talented Child*, Harper Collins, Sydney, 1995

McGrath, H. *Friendly Kids, Friendly Classrooms*, Longmans, Melbourne, 1991

McGrath, H. *Dirty Tricks*, Longmans, Melbourne, 1999

Mullinar, G. *Not just Four-letter Words*, Harper Collins, Sydney, 1994

Pinker, S. *How the Mind Works*, Penguin Books, London, 1997

Prosser, B. *ADHD: Who's failing who?* Finch Publishing, Sydney, 2005

Sheridan, S. *Tough Kids: Social skills program*, Sopris West, Silvereye Distribution, Newcastle, 1996

Van der Kley, M. *Social Skills and Anger Management: a 10-session course for 7- to 12-year-olds*, Silvereye Distribution, Newcastle, 1997

Wallace, I. *You and your A.D.D. Child*, Harper Collins, Sydney, 1996

Wilson, C. *Room 14, social language program*, Lingui Systems, Silvereye Distribution, Newcastle, 1993

York, P., York, D. & Wachtel, T. *Tough Love*, Bantam, NY, 1982

Zimbardo, P. *The Shy Child*, Doubleday, Dolphin, NY, 1981

Other Finch titles of interest

Raising Girls
Why girls are different – and how to help them grow up happy and strong – Gisela Preuschoff
Gisela Preuschoff injects her own experiences as mother of four into this book, and illustrates her points with stories and examples from the experiences of many families. Her advice ranges from birth to late adolescence – and across physical and sexual development, schools and learning, gender stereotyping, parent–child relationships and the daughter's emotional life. ISBN 978 1876451 592

Adolescence
A guide for parents – Michael Carr-Gregg and Erin Shale
In this informative and wide-ranging book, the authors help parents understand what is happening for young people aged 10–20 and how to deal with it. They discuss the big questions in a young person's life and provide parents and teachers with useful approaches for handling problems. ISBN 978 1876451 356

A Handbook for Happy Families
A practical and fun-filled guide to managing children's behaviour – Dr John Irvine
In this wise and humorous approach to parenting, the author tackles the commonest problems with children of all ages. He also presents his innovative and well-tested 'Happy/sad face discipline system', which draws families together rather than dividing them. ISBN 978 1876451 417

Raising Boys
Why boys are different – and how to help them become happy and well-balanced men (2nd edition) – Steve Biddulph
In his international bestseller, Steve Biddulph examines the crucial ways that boys differ from girls. He looks at boys' development from birth to manhood and discusses the warm, strong parenting and guidance boys need. ISBN 978 1876451 509

Confident Parenting
How to set limits, be considerate and stay in charge – Dr William Doherty
'We may be the most child-sensitive generations of parents the world has ever known – and the most confused and insecure,' says the author. This book shows you how to parent effectively and how to ensure that your family is not overwhelmed by external pressures such as advertising, TV, and peer culture. ISBN 978 1876451 462

Fathering from the Fast Lane
Practical ideas for busy dads – Dr Bruce Robinson
The pressures of working life today mean that many fathers are not spending the time with their children that they would like. This book presents practical and straightforward ways to improve this situation. In this collection of valuable fathering ideas, over 75 men from various backgrounds speak about how they balance demanding jobs with being a good dad. ISBN 978 1876451 219

Parenting after Separation
Making the most of family changes – Jill Burrett
So much parenting now takes place from two households, following separation. This book offers positive approaches to helping children and making the most of these family changes. ISBN 978 1876451 370

Bully Blocking
Six secrets to help children deal with teasing and bullying –Evelyn Field
Bully Blocking, a fully revised edition of the highly successful **Bully Busting**, offers practical advice to help children (aged 4 –16) deal with bullies who tease, exclude, intimidate or harass. Renowned bullying specialist Evelyn Field provides parents and teachers with understandings and tested approaches to assist a child who is a target or a bully. ISBN 978 1876451 776

Tricky Kids
Transforming conflict and freeing their potential – Andrew Fuller
Clinical psychologist Andrew Fuller pulls together his immense counselling experience and easy-to-read style in examining the behaviour of 'tricky kids'. In his easy-to-read style he identifies six different types of tricky kids and leads parents through a five-step program designed to help turn the attitude of these kids around so they can achieve their potential. ISBN 978 1876451 769

Manhood
An action plan for changing men's lives (3rd edition) –Steve Biddulph
Steve Biddulph tackles the key areas of a man's life – parenting, love and sexuality, finding meaning in work, and making real friends. He presents new pathways to healing the past and forming true partnerships with women, as well as honouring our own inner needs. ISBN 978 1876451 202

On Their Own
Boys growing up underfathered – Rex McCann
For a young man, growing up without an involved father in his life can leave a powerful sense of loss. *On Their Own* considers the needs of young men as they mature, the passage from boyhood to manhood, and the roles of fathers and mothers. ISBN 1876451 080

Fear-free Children
Dr Janet Hall – Dr Janet Hall draws on real-life case studies to help parents overcome specific fears and anxieties that their children have, such as fear of the dark, fear of being alone or fear of animals. ISBN 987 1876451 233

Fight-free Families
Dr Janet Hall – Dr Janet Hall provides solutions to conflicts in a wide range of family ages and situations, from young children through to adolescents. ISBN 978 1876451 226

Easy Parenting
Ken and Elizabeth Mellor Ken and Elizabeth Mellor offer many practical skills and approaches, including different ways of loving your child; using repetition to help children learn; developing your child's self-esteem; struggling with children for their benefit; managing conflicts between siblings; and effective ways to discipline. ISBN 978 1876451 110
For further information on these and all of our titles, visit our website: www.finch.com.au

Index